✧ ✦ ✧ ✦ ✧ ✦ ✧ ✦ ✧ ✦ ✧ ✦ ✧ ✦ ✧ ✦

BASEBALL SUPERSTARS

Randy Johnson

✦ ✧ ✦ ✧ ✦ ✧ ✦ ✧ ✦ ✧ ✦ ✧ ✦ ✧ ✦ ✧

Hank Aaron

Ty Cobb

Lou Gehrig

Derek Jeter

Randy Johnson

Mike Piazza

Kirby Puckett

Jackie Robinson

Ichiro Suzuki

Bernie Williams

BASEBALL
SUPERSTARS

Randy Johnson

Susan Muaddi Darraj
and Rob Maaddi

CHELSEA HOUSE
PUBLISHERS
An imprint of Infobase Publishing

RANDY JOHNSON

Chelsea House
An imprint of Infobase Publishing
132 West 31st Street
New York NY 10001

Library of Congress Cataloging-in-Publication Data
Darraj, Susan Muaddi.
 Randy Johnson / Susan Muaddi Darraj and Rob Maaddi.
   p. cm. — (Baseball superstars)
 Includes bibliographical references and index.
 ISBN-13: 978-0-7910-9441-9 (hardcover)
 ISBN-10: 0-7910-9441-3 (hardcover)
 1. Johnson, Randy, 1963- 2. Baseball players—United States—Biography.
3. Pitchers (Baseball)—United States—Biography. 4. New York Yankees
(Baseball team) I. Maaddi, Rob. II. Title. III. Series.
 GV865.J599D37 2007
 796.357092—dc22
 [B]   2007006221

Series design by Erik Lindstrom
Cover design by Ben Peterson

Printed in the United States of America

Bang EJB 10 9 8 7 6 5 4 3 2 1

This book is printed on acid-free paper.

CONTENTS

New York,
New York

It was eight o'clock in the morning on Monday, January 10, 2005, in Midtown Manhattan, when Randy Johnson emerged from the front doors of the Four Seasons hotel. The day was going to be a busy one. First he had to visit the doctor's office for a general physical evaluation. Wearing a gray sweat suit, he would soon be wearing the navy-blue pinstripes of New York's most successful baseball team; it was his first week as an official member of the famous New York Yankees.

Just a couple of weeks earlier, on December 30, 2004, he signed an agreement with the Yankees to join the club. The deal earned him $32 million for two years, until the 2007 season. To acquire Johnson, the Yankees had traded three players—pitchers Javier Vázquez and Brad Halsey and catcher Dioner

"Get out of my face; that's all I ask," Randy Johnson said on January 10, 2005, in Manhattan as he tried to block a WCBS-TV cameraman from taking his picture. Johnson was on his way to get his physical after being traded from the Arizona Diamondbacks to the New York Yankees. Johnson's introduction to New York's fans and media was not an encouraging one.

Navarro—and given $9 million to Johnson's former team, the Arizona Diamondbacks.

At the time of the acquisition, Yankee fans were split about the decision: Some people were thrilled that Johnson, one of the most intimidating and successful pitchers in professional baseball, was playing on their side, while others speculated that Johnson was past his prime. He was 41 years old, an age that is considered to be well past the time when a player's abilities start to decline. He also had a history of back problems. Nevertheless, people were excited to see how the "Big Unit," as Johnson was known because of his height (6-foot-10, or 208 centimeters), would fare in New York City, where fans take their sports seriously and follow the Yankees very closely.

As Johnson headed down Madison Avenue, accompanied by members of the Yankees' security team, he encountered reporters and cameramen. Vinny Everett, a cameraman with WCBS-TV, tried to film him, while WCBS reporter Duke Castiglione tried to get a statement, but Johnson became annoyed. He put his hand up to the video camera and snapped, "Get out of my face; that's all I ask." One of the security team members told the reporter, "No cameras," but the video continued to roll.

Exasperated, Johnson yelled, "Don't get in my face. I don't care who you are. Don't get in my face." When Everett protested that he just wanted to get a shot, Johnson retorted, "Don't get in my face, and don't talk back to me, all right?"

At the corner of Madison Avenue and 59th Street, he stopped and snapped at *New York Daily News* photographer Michael Schwartz: "Look, don't take my picture." He added, "Don't follow me. Don't follow me."

"Come on, Randy," pleaded Everett, the cameraman. Johnson responded threateningly: "Or you'll see what I'm like!" As Johnson stormed away, Everett shouted, "Welcome to New York!"

News reports that day and the next were ablaze with headlines about Johnson's behavior. News stations replayed the videotape over and over, showing Johnson putting his long arm up to the camera lens, blocking the cameraman's view, and yelling angrily at the reporters. The video was also posted on the Internet, where millions of people saw it and circulated it.

The *New York Daily News* promptly announced: "The Big Unit is officially New York's biggest $32 million crybaby." The Associated Press sarcastically wrote, "Hey, Randy, welcome to

☆ ☆ ☆ ☆ ☆

JOHNSON'S KILLER FASTBALL

Randy Johnson always heard he had a killer fastball. Unfortunately, it turned out to be true.

In March 2001, Johnson was on the mound during one of his final outings in spring training when he accidentally hit and killed a dove flying in front of home plate.

The Arizona Diamondbacks were playing the San Francisco Giants in Tucson, Arizona. Calvin Murray was at the plate in the seventh inning to bat against Johnson. The 95-mile-per-hour (153-kilometer-per-hour) pitch never made it to catcher Rod Barajas's mitt. Instead, it struck the bird, which landed a few feet from the plate amid a sea of feathers.

Barajas told The Associated Press: "I'm sitting there waiting for it, and I'm expecting to catch the thing, and all you see is an explosion. It's crazy. There's still feathers down there."

Johnson took the incident quite seriously. "I didn't think it was all that funny," he told AP.

Murray could not believe what had happened. He said the pitch should have been called a ball, but it was ruled no pitch. "The bird just exploded. Feathers everywhere. Poof!" Murray said in the AP story.

Giants second baseman Jeff Kent picked up the dead bird with his bare hands and jokingly pointed toward Johnson before taking it to the dugout. The game continued.

This was not the first time a bird was killed by a baseball thrown by a major leaguer. In August 1983, New York Yankees outfielder Dave Winfield killed a seagull in Toronto with a

New York!" Back in Arizona, the skirmish also made headlines: The *Arizona Republic*'s article on the incident was entitled, "Talk to the Hand: Unit Pitches a Fit." In the article, sportswriter Bob

☆ ☆ ☆ ☆ ☆

warm-up throw. The police charged him with animal cruelty, but the charge was later dropped.

"This was a little more dramatic," Diamondbacks manager Bob Brenly told AP. "I can honestly say I have never seen that before."

Reporter Murray Campbell sought to find the likelihood of such an occurrence, so he interviewed some practitioners of probability theory for his article in the *Globe and Mail* of Toronto, Canada. Jeffrey Rosenthal, a Harvard-trained University of Toronto professor, calculated that the chances of Johnson killing the dove with his pitch were one in 13 million.

Campbell explained in his article:

Certain assumptions are made, first that there are 100 doves in the square kilometer around the Tucson ballpark. It is also assumed that they are flying in no apparent pattern with no partic-ular attraction or repulsion related to baseball-stadium smells—sweat, pine tar, peanuts, spilled beer, or even Murray's after-shave. Next, Rosenthal had to guess the diameter of a dove's body and of a baseball to calculate the volume of space where a dove could be hit by a pitch. There are no birds or balls in his office, so each is assumed to be about 10 centimeters in diameter. The distance between the pitcher's rubber and home plate—always stated as 60 feet 6 inches—is put down as roughly 18 meters. After that, it's simple work—for Rosenthal, at least—to calculate that Johnson's pitch was a one-in-13-million thing.

Young wrote, "It didn't take long for Randy Johnson to unveil his menacing intimidation act on New York—and he hasn't even picked up a baseball yet."

Sportswriters, analysts, and fans agreed that Johnson deserved a certain level of privacy, but they knew that New York's fast-paced, news-hungry environment was radically different from the more mellow atmosphere of Phoenix, Arizona. Having just signed a $32 million contract with the Yankees, Johnson would not be excused or exempted from media attention.

APOLOGIES

Later the same day, Johnson issued a statement to the press, apologizing for his behavior. Through the Yankees' press office, he said, "I hope that everyone will understand that the past few days have been a bit overwhelming and I wish I had handled the situation differently. I am very sorry it happened."

The next day, Johnson appeared at a news conference that had been scheduled earlier to announce that the deal with the Diamondbacks had been finalized. Johnson knew that he had to make things right with New York's fans and media. According to an article by *New York Daily News* writer Sam Borden, he apologized right away: "The situation [on Monday], it was unprofessional," he said. "Obviously I feel very foolish today at such a great moment of my career that I would have to stand before you and apologize for my actions. Hopefully it's water under the bridge. I'm sorry. . . . I hope I can move on and get another chance to prove that I'm worth coming here."

By the time the news conference aired, however, the media had reminded baseball fans in New York and across the country that the incident in Manhattan was hardly the first time Johnson had been involved in a confrontation. For example, during the 2004 season with the Diamondbacks, Johnson provoked a fight with Luis Gonzalez, a teammate who had dropped

Randy Johnson smiled during a news conference on January 11, 2005, the day after his run-in with the media on a Manhattan street. He apologized for his behavior, saying, "I hope I can move on and get another chance to prove that I'm worth coming here."

a fly ball that led to the team's loss. In the dugout, Johnson apparently made a comment to Gonzalez about the error and the two nearly had a fight. Reports stated that Johnson pushed his teammate into a watercooler.

In response to reporters' questions at the Yankee news conference, Johnson added, "I suppose a lot of things are new to me here. . . . I'm not used to having photographers pop out from behind the bushes and take my picture or things like that. Do I have to get used to that? Without a doubt."

Nevertheless, New York Yankees fans wondered if the Big Unit would be able to adapt and survive in the Big Apple.

A Born Basketball Star?

Walnut Creek, California, is a small town but one that supports and promotes sports, especially for its youth. Randall David Johnson was born there on September 10, 1963. His parents, Carol and Rollen Johnson, had five other children, and Randall, soon nicknamed Randy, was the baby of the clan.

Rollen Johnson, who towered over most of his peers at 6 feet 6 inches (198 centimeters) tall, was a police officer. Shortly after their youngest son was born, Rollen (whose family and friends called him "Bud") and Carol moved the family to Livermore, California—a town not too far from Walnut Creek in the San Francisco Bay area. Randy attended elementary school in Livermore, but he grew up feeling like an outcast. The reason was his height—he grew so quickly that by the time he was 12 years old, he was almost 6 feet tall (183 centimeters). In his family, such height was hardly unusual—after all, Randy's father and brothers were also quite tall.

Randy, though, had a tough time getting used to always being the tallest kid in his class. To try to fit in with his classmates, he resorted to joking around. Before long, he was known as the class clown. His clowning around often got him into trouble, however, especially when it disrupted classes or upset his teachers. "I was in the principal's office a lot," he once said, "because I was kind of loud in the classroom, making jokes and disrupting the class."

Randy always thought he would grow up to be a police officer like his father. Because Bud and Carol Johnson were concerned about his conduct, however, they wanted their son to understand teamwork. They encouraged him to join sports teams, knowing that the discipline required by the games would help him to control his behavior. Playing sports would also provide him with the self-confidence he needed to understand that his height could be used to his advantage, instead of being a liability.

In 1972, he joined Little League, but his first day was a disaster because he arrived late and could not find his team. As his entry on JockBio.com relates:

> The 8-year-old grabbed his glove and walked over to tryouts at the local athletic complex. When he got there he saw more than a hundred kids spread out over half a dozen diamonds. He did not recognize any friends or classmates, and a lot of the boys looked older. He wasn't sure he had the right paperwork or ID, and ran home in tears. Carol walked Randy back to tryouts and got him signed up. He was soon playing many different sports, and his brothers helped him to enjoy the games and practice his skills.

According to Matt Christopher, author of *On the Mound with Randy Johnson*, "Bud was the first person to realize that his son might have a special talent" for baseball. Randy knew immediately that he wanted to play just one position: pitcher.

☆ ☆ ☆ ☆ ☆
GIVING BACK TO THE COMMUNITY

Randy Johnson's relentless practice of throwing strikes against the garage door as a young boy would pay off for him in the years to come. It would pay off in philanthropic ways as well. Through Johnson's "Strikeout Homelessness" program, Johnson pledges to donate $1,000 per victory and $100 per strikeout to charities and organizations that help the homeless in the communities where he plays. So far in his career, he has donated more than $300,000 to fight homelessness.

Johnson has also been quite active in fundraising for the Cystic Fibrosis Foundation, having raised more than $1 million over the past several years. As one fundraising benefit for the foundation, he holds a golf tournament each year. For his efforts, the Arizona chapter of the Cystic Fibrosis Foundation named him the recipient of its Bronze Sierra award in 1999. The award is given annually to a person who has made a significant contribution to trying to find a cure for cystic fibrosis.

Johnson's philanthropy covers a wide range of areas. After a tsunami swept across the Indian Ocean in late 2004, killing hundreds of thousands of people in Southeast Asia, Johnson made a $400,000 donation to the relief efforts of the American Red Cross. He has also provided, through his contract with Nike, thousands of pairs of footwear to needy people. Johnson supports the Salvation Army and the Make-a-Wish Foundation, too.

He could throw the baseball well—and he could throw it hard, which intimidated the batters and got them to strike out.

Randy practiced pitching by creating a "strikeout zone" with tape on his garage door and throwing a tennis ball at it. His pitches were so hard that he often loosened the nails in the door. His father would hammer the nails back in after his son's pitching sessions were over. Often, after working his day job, Bud Johnson would put on a mitt and play catcher to Randy's pitches.

Randy also enjoyed playing basketball. He was so tall that rebounding the ball and making shots were easier for him than for his teammates. Soon, Randy came to consider basketball and baseball his favorite sports because he truly excelled at them.

When he attended Livermore High School, Randy, who had reached 6 feet 7 inches (201 centimeters) tall and was still growing, naturally played for the school's sports teams, and the coaches were pleased to have such a talent. He was a member of the junior-varsity basketball team as a freshman, and he played well. Despite his towering height, he displayed excellent coordination and finesse on the court.

CUT FROM THE TEAM

When he entered the tenth grade, Randy hoped to make the varsity basketball team. He encountered a setback, however. The varsity coach rigidly enforced a rule that all players on the varsity team be able to run a mile in less than seven minutes. He felt that speed and endurance were essential to playing well on the basketball court. Unfortunately, Randy was not a gifted runner. According to Matt Christopher, "Randy just couldn't do it. He ran well for short periods of time, but he was so tall and gangly, he just didn't yet have enough stamina to run a mile so quickly." He failed the test.

Randy was cut from the team, which devastated him. This misfortune, however, made him turn seriously to the sport of baseball, and he received a lot of encouragement from his coaches. In his junior year, he again tried out for the varsity basketball team and again did not make the squad because he still could not run the mile in less than seven minutes. Again, he focused on baseball.

So it was in high school that Randy decided to concentrate exclusively on baseball and was encouraged to believe he could make a career out of it. He became known for his pitching skills, which were not always excellent. He had speed but not always control. Still, he did have his glorious moments on the mound. He was a left-handed pitcher, and he threw in a sidearm style, which made him a rarity. His style allowed him to pack a lot of momentum into his pitches, so that the ball, upon release, headed toward home plate at an alarming speed.

He still presented an unusual sight on the mound. Tall and skinny, Randy was the oddest-looking baseball player anyone had ever seen. Opposing players, scouts, and friends alike nicknamed him "Ichabod Crane," after the unusual and awkward main character in Washington Irving's story "The Legend of Sleepy Hollow." Randy felt as tormented on the mound as Irving's character had felt—he thought everyone was staring at him, and usually he was right.

The taunting was difficult for him to endure. He said, "I started getting noticed a lot because of my height. I felt like I was in a three-ring circus and didn't know how to handle it." His father, though, encouraged him to focus on his athletic ability and to keep practicing; Bud believed his son could one day play in the major leagues and become a professional baseball star. He knew that the combination of Randy's height, pitching skills, and talent were rare.

Years later, Randy remembered how his father motivated him: "No one else ever sat me down and said, 'You've got all the potential in the world.' My dad did that." His father's encouragement helped Randy to ignore the taunts as best he could.

Randy Johnson embraced his mother, Carol, before a December 1998 news conference to announce that he had signed with the Arizona Diamondbacks. Johnson's mother and his father, Bud, encouraged Randy to get involved in sports so he would learn the value of team-work. They also believed that participating in sports would help Randy feel less self-conscious about his height.

THE LIVERMORE COWBOYS

Luckily for Johnson, the Livermore Cowboys got a new coach during his junior year who believed in Randy's skills and talent as much as his father did.

Coach Eric Hoff had heard about the teenager who stood well over six-and-a-half feet tall and could throw a fastball at 90 miles per hour (145 kilometers per hour). He also knew that Randy did not have great control; he threw well, but often pitches got away from him and he ended up walking a lot of batters.

The fastball was Randy's only real pitch. He did not know how to throw anything else. "He definitely had a lot of talent, a live arm," Hoff said in *On the Mound with Randy Johnson*. "He didn't have the mentality of a pitcher, but he had the tools."

Part of the problem was Randy's height, although it also made him a good pitcher. Taller pitchers have more strength and range, and therefore they can throw the ball harder than a shorter pitcher. Their height, however, also makes it difficult for them to control their pitches. As Matt Christopher explains: "The taller a pitcher is, the more difficulty he often has with his windup and delivery, what scouts and coaches call 'mechanics.' To succeed, a pitcher must throw exactly the same way each and every time. It's hard for a tall pitcher to do that." (Furthermore, as Johnson would discover later, taller pitchers ended up placing more strain on their backs because of the long range of their arms and legs.)

The coach wanted Randy to think smart, like a pitcher, and to be able to throw a variety of pitches, depending on the strength of the batter he was facing. For example, a pitcher might throw different pitches to a left-handed batter than he would to a right-handed batter. Hoff helped Randy develop two new pitches: a curveball and a changeup. A curveball is a pitch that suddenly veers in a different direction from where it was thrown; for example, Randy, a left-handed pitcher, would throw a curveball that would suddenly move to the right. A changeup is a pitch that deceives the batter because it looks like a fastball but is thrown at a slower speed; therefore, the batter swings too early and misses the ball.

Soon, Randy was throwing more controlled pitches. He struck out more batters. His team, though, was not too good, so he ended up losing many games—about as many as he won, in fact.

Bud Johnson attended almost every game that Randy played and offered his son advice afterward, as well as tips on how to throw better in the next game. No matter how well Randy did, Bud Johnson reminded him that he could improve. Randy relied on his father's advice and encouragement and took what his father said to heart. He learned to be a perfectionist and to always try to be the best.

Other people started to attend Randy's games: scouts. In most sports, scouts search for new, raw talent at the high school and college levels to determine who may have a shot at the professional leagues. Scouts had heard about the gangly pitcher with the fiery fastball, and they began to watch his performances at the Livermore games.

In 1982, in his last game for his high school team, he pitched a perfect game, in which he allowed no hits, no walks, and no runs. He struck out 13 batters. Many scouts were in the stands, and they were quite impressed by what they had seen. Randy's perfect game was a grand achievement, one that seemed to be a good omen for his career after high school. His senior year had been impressive overall: in $66^{1}/_{3}$ innings of pitching, he struck out 121 batters.

University Years

When he graduated, Randy Johnson had a chance to play professional baseball right away. The Atlanta Braves took him in the third round of the draft. To be drafted at such a young age was an opportunity that most baseball hopefuls would have seized without question, but Randy, his parents, and coach Eric Hoff mulled over the decision.

Although Randy was a great pitcher with a lot of talent, he still had to overcome his inconsistency. He still threw a lot of wild pitches, which caused him to walk many batters. Hoff felt that, if Randy went into professional baseball right away, he would have a tough time because his coaches would push him to win, rather than help him perfect his skills. Essentially, Hoff and the Johnsons decided that Randy was just not ready—not yet.

Instead, Randy decided to attend college. He knew he could earn a degree as well as polish his pitching skills while playing for a university team. To his parents, as Matt Christopher writes, "a college education was worth more than sixty thousand dollars," which was the amount of the signing bonus the Braves were offering their son.

He wanted to attend the University of Southern California (USC), which had a strong sports tradition and which offered him an athletic scholarship. The scholarship, though, was for basketball, not baseball, and it was only a partial scholarship.

At the same time, another university had offered Randy a full baseball scholarship. Coach Hoff contacted USC and told the university to make a better offer or Randy would attend the other school. USC did, finally offering Randy a full scholarship for baseball and basketball.

Excited, Randy began his college career in the fall of 1982 at USC and earned a spot as a pitcher on the baseball team. He had a tough time, however, adjusting to college life. "He was homesick," writes Matt Christopher, "having trouble in his classes, lonely, and trying to absorb all the advice he got from the Trojan coaching staff." The Trojans' coach, Rod Dedeaux, worked with him closely, but Randy was very emotional.

Indeed, Randy had developed a reputation as a "flake," according to Larry Stone, who wrote a biography of the pitcher, *Randy Johnson: Arizona Heat!* "He often talked to himself on the mound and gestured wildly after big plays," Stone writes. He was very intense and eager, and he got upset when things went wrong.

One episode during his college career illustrates how Randy's intensity could cause him to be off the mark. "As a freshman, in his collegiate debut against Stanford," Stone writes, "he entered the game in relief. When he got to the mound, he told Dedeaux that he planned to pitch from the stretch to hold the base runner close to first base. Dedeaux gently informed him that there was no runner at first base; the person he was looking at was Stanford's first-base coach."

His actions caught the attention of his teammates, according to Matt Christopher:

> He would get so intense that several innings after making a bad pitch he would still be muttering to himself about it. Sometimes when the ball was hit, Randy would race over to first base and make calls just like the umpire. In between pitches he sometimes talked to the baseball and yelled at the hitters. His teammates thought Randy was a real character.

ERRATIC ON THE MOUND

In his early years, his pitching prowess was random at best—he could strike out an amazing number of batters, but he often threw wild pitches. His coaches never knew if he would be in control when he started on the mound or if he would let his pitches get away from him.

In his first year with the Trojans, when he was a freshman, the coaches used him as a relief pitcher, toward the middle or end of the game when the starting pitcher was removed. He recorded five wins and three saves, which was a good, though not great, record. However, as Matt Christopher writes, he "struck out only 34 hitters in 47 innings. His earned-run average, the average number of runs a pitcher gives up per every nine innings, was over five. Under two is considered great, under three very good, and under four is OK." To have an ERA over five was bad news: He was allowing too many batters to hit the ball, get on base, and score.

To get him to pitch more consistently, the Trojans offered him excellent coaching and plenty of support. Randy's parents and Randy himself knew he had made a wise decision to go to college first, rather than join the majors. He would be worth more to a team in the major leagues once he could control

Rod Dedeaux *(right)*, the longtime baseball coach at the University of Southern California, instructs a player in this March 1970 photograph. He was Randy Johnson's coach at USC, and he worked closely with Johnson—on the pitcher's technique and his composure.

his pitching arm. (One of his Trojan teammates was Mark McGwire, who would later become a power hitter in baseball, playing for the Oakland Athletics and the St. Louis Cardinals.)

In his sophomore year, Randy improved greatly. The Trojans allowed Randy to start games as a pitcher. In eight games, he won five and lost three. More important, his ERA dropped to 3.35. In 78 innings, he struck out 73 batters and only allowed 72 hits. He still walked 52 batters, however.

In his junior year at USC, Randy set a Trojan record—unfortunately, it was a record no one would want to hold. He walked 104 batters during the season, the most ever in Trojan history. Also, his ERA was 5.32.

"I was a true wild man in college," he recalls in Stone's book. "I'd walk two guys, then strike out the side. I was raw."

In an interview with a reporter during his college days, he said, "It's frustrating. I'm throwing better this season, but I'm pitching in spurts. I'm not consistent like you have to

★ ★ ★ ★ ★

THE SHUTTERBUG

Randy Johnson's interest in photography blossomed while he was at the University of Southern California. Photography had been a weekend hobby for Johnson when he was growing up. While at USC, he went to the school newspaper, the *Daily Trojan*, and was asked to shoot some pictures. So began a regular gig. Many of his assignments were standard ones: student life, political campaigns, speakers who visited campus. Combining his love of photography and music, Johnson scooped up the assignments to shoot concerts—photographing bands at clubs like the Roxy and the Viper Room. "They would ask me to go, because they knew I enjoyed shooting that kind of stuff," Johnson said in a 2002 article in the *Daily Trojan*.

In the interview, Johnson said that his work with a camera had a connection to his work on the mound. "I feel there's a great correlation of pitching to photography," he said. "You have to stay in focus. Looking at the viewfinder is like looking at the strike zone."

be in pro ball. I'm giving up too many walks and you can't do that."

While his control may have been erratic on the ball field, Randy was finding ways to relax elsewhere on the USC campus. He discovered a love of photography and music. He became a photographer for the school paper, the *Daily Trojan*. He spent a lot of his free time roaming the campus, looking for interesting shots and angles. In fact, he decided to major in fine arts to develop his skills. He also continued an

☆ ☆ ☆ ☆ ☆ ☆

He continued to pursue photography during the 1980s, and in 1990, some of his work was displayed in the Art Expo '90 exhibition in Los Angeles. As his baseball stardom grew, the photography got away from him, although his interest has not waned. "I've become friends with a lot of photographers from the *Sporting News, Sports Illustrated*— all because of my interest in that field," he said in the *Daily Trojan* article.

Still, he picks up a camera when he can. In 1996, when he was out for most of the season with a back injury, a reporter for *USA Today* caught him peering through the lens. At a game in Baltimore, he was taking a picture of shortstops Cal Ripken, Jr., and Alex Rodriguez reading *Superman* and *Superboy* comics. The shot was going to be reproduced on a card. "I like taking pictures on the road," Johnson said in the *USA Today* article. "It takes the edge away when things are going good or bad."

interest in drumming; as a teenager, he had played with a group of friends in an amateur band, usually in someone's garage. Randy was able to relax by hitting the drums and enjoying the rhythm.

By his third year with the Trojans, major-league scouts showed a lot of interest in Randy Johnson. Despite being inconsistent, he had an excellent, powerful fastball that was clocked at more than 90 miles per hour (145 kilometers per hour) and that could intimidate many batters. Scouts considered him a hot prospect. In fact, the magazine *Baseball America*, which covers college and minor-league ball, rated him in 1985 as the fourth-best pitcher in the country.

Randy, his coaches, and his parents were confident that he would get an excellent offer from a major-league team.

The Big
Leagues

In June 1985, Randy Johnson was taken by the Montreal Expos in the second round of the draft. He was disappointed not to have been drafted in the first round, which was when the top prospects were chosen. The second round was still great, however, and he was excited.

The major-league teams have a minor-league farm system in which they develop new talent for their ball clubs. These minor-league clubs are divided into four classes: Rookie, Single A, Double A, and Triple A. Triple A is the highest level: The players who are moved to the Triple-A leagues can usually expect to be called up to the majors.

When Johnson signed with the Expos, however, he was assigned to one of the Expos' A-level minor-league teams— Jamestown of the New York–Penn League. He was even more upset soon after he started, when he developed a sore arm from pitching. His season record was a dismal 0 wins and 3 losses. His ERA, that all-important number, was 5.93.

Johnson had a reputation for being a pitcher who struck out batters regularly, but he was not thought to be spectacular, especially in comparison with other pitchers that season. Determined to succeed, Johnson became dedicated to improving his pitching performance during the off-season.

Johnson's height and the speed of his fastball were quite intimidating. Many batters knew how hard he could throw the fastball, and the thought of it made them shudder. In addition, Johnson's personality was far from friendly. When he pitched, he meant business. Once, during a game, Johnson threw a pitch way over the batter's head. Furious, the batter headed toward the mound to confront Johnson; Johnson's teammate, pitcher Brian Holman, recalls that Johnson pointed at the approaching batter and warned him, "Don't come out here, or I'll take your life." The batter quickly retreated, and the game resumed.

In 1986, his second minor-league season, Johnson pitched for another Single-A-level team, West Palm Beach in the Florida State League. His record was 8–7 while his ERA dropped to 3.16. Johnson was progressing well enough that the Expos moved him up to their Double-A team, Jacksonville of the Southern League, in 1987. He began to work with pitching coach Joe Kerrigan, whose experience and tips proved invaluable. A tall man himself at 6-foot-5 (196 centimeters), Kerrigan understood that Johnson's problems were an issue of mechanics—the way in which he threw the ball, how he landed during the pitching motion, at which angle he released the ball, and other factors.

Kerrigan worked carefully with Johnson, helping him to pay attention to how and when he released the ball. Slowly, his pitching began to improve as he gained more and more control over his arm. Johnson won 11 games that season, and he struck out a league-high 163 batters in 140 innings.

Pitching coach Joe Kerrigan observed Randy Johnson as he pitched batting practice in February 2006 during the Yankees' spring training in Tampa, Florida. Johnson and Kerrigan went way back—Kerrigan worked with Johnson on his mechanics in 1987, when they both were with the Montreal Expos' Double-AA farm team in Jacksonville, Florida.

The next season, Johnson was more ready than ever to impress the ball club—he was determined to move up to the majors as soon as possible. He did move up to the Triple-A team, the Indianapolis Indians, a step away from where he wanted to be. (Kerrigan, his faithful coach, was also promoted in recognition of how much progress he had made with the team's biggest pitching prospect.)

Larry Stone writes that, despite his impending success, Johnson was still upset by references to his height. Every player he encountered was shorter than he was, and fans, coaches, and fellow ballplayers alike constantly mentioned his 6-foot-10-inch frame. "As was the case in high school and college," Stone writes, "Randy often felt like a freak on display." This was especially true when the public-address announcer at games introduced him to the crowd as "the world's tallest pitcher."

A CLOSE CALL

In mid-June 1988, Johnson received exciting news: After his next game, he would be joining the Expos. Although Johnson was still an inconsistent thrower, the Expos felt he was ready to pitch in the major leagues. They were in the midst of a tight division race and thought that it was time to call up fresh talent. With his height and intimidating presence on the mound, Johnson seemed to be just the person to help them out.

Then Johnson did something that nearly caused him to ruin the opportunity he had craved for so long.

During what would have been his last game in the Triple-A minors, he lost control. The game had been going well, and then he threw a fastball to the batter. The batter connected with the ball, smacking it right back toward the mound, right at Johnson. Instinctively, Johnson threw his arm in front of his face, except he used his bare hand—his pitching hand—rather than the gloved one. The ball struck his left wrist sharply, and he collapsed to the dirt.

Nearly in tears, he headed to the dugout to have a doctor examine his wrist. From the pain and swelling, Johnson was sure it was broken. He was also sure that his major-league career, within his grasp, had been snatched away from him in a cruel twist of fate.

Johnson allowed his emotions to take over. As he passed by a wooden bat rack hanging on the wall, he reached out and punched it with his right hand. Of course, this hurt—but he did not care because he was so angry.

When the doctors examined X-rays of his hands, however, they discovered that his left hand, which he used to throw, was actually fine. His wrist was bruised, and he would need only a week to recover from that injury. His right hand, though, which had nearly broken the wooden bat rack, was the one that was really injured. Johnson had broken a bone in that hand that would require six weeks to heal.

According to Matt Christopher, "The Expos were angry with him. By allowing his emotions to take over, Randy had not only harmed himself, he had hurt Montreal's chances of winning the division." (The team ended up finishing in third place in the National League East, with an 81–81 record.)

Johnson did not yet understand that he played for a ball club—that every action he took or lack of action had a rippling effect on his team. He had to think like a professional in order to play like one.

The Expos soon established what it called "The Randy Johnson Rule." The Expos posted signs in the clubhouses of all their minor-league teams. The signs stated bluntly, "Anybody who does something hasty to inhibit his ability will be fined."

When his hand healed, Johnson rejoined his Triple-A team. His season ended fairly well, with an 8–7 record and a 3.26 ERA. The team won the minor-league American Association championships, which was partially a result of Johnson's solid pitching.

The Expos finally gave him another chance and called him up to the majors.

THE BIG UNIT

Johnson started his first game in the major leagues on September 15, 1988. As he took to the mound, he made history, officially becoming the world's tallest baseball player at 6 feet 10 inches, breaking the previous record set by Johnny Gee, who was one inch shorter.

Johnson was interested in making history for reasons other than his height. He pitched his first game against the Pittsburgh Pirates, and he won despite giving up two home runs to Glenn Wilson. He went on to win three of his first four starts.

He did well in that first month in the major leagues, finishing with an ERA of 2.42. As he expected, though, he became known as a pitcher who lacked total control on the mound. He often threw wild pitches and still walked many batters, marking him as an unreliable force.

His teammates continued to comment about his height. One day, while running sprints during training, outfielder Tim Raines almost ran right into Johnson. "Man," Raines said, "you're a big unit, aren't you?" From that moment on, the nickname "Big Unit" stuck to Johnson.

He worked hard in the off-season, hoping to come back strong for his first full season with the Expos. "It took me a while to get control of my body, to find a delivery that would keep my arms and legs in sync with the rest of me," he told the media. "But I'm ready now."

However, he was not. The 1989 season started badly for Johnson. He was walking way too many batters. In fact, he was walking almost one batter an inning. The Expos were intent on winning the pennant that year, and they were annoyed with Johnson's inability to throw consistently. The team managers felt that the Expos could not depend on him. After compiling a 6.69 ERA in his first six games, they sent him down to the minor leagues again to work on his pitching. He pitched three games for Indianapolis. At the end of May 1989, however, the Expos traded Johnson to the Seattle Mariners, even though a year earlier the Expos had told other teams that he was "untouchable" and would never be let go. Now they let him go in order to acquire pitcher Mark Langston.

The Big Unit was headed for Washington State.

Even though he was drafted by the Montreal Expos, Randy Johnson ended up playing only a short time on the team—in September 1988 and for the first two months of the 1989 season. Then, he was traded to the Seattle Mariners.

IN A MARINER UNIFORM

Most baseball experts agree that it was in Seattle that Johnson began to demonstrate his real power as a pitcher.

The Mariners were a relatively new team; established in 1977, the ball club struggled for its first few years with new players and raw talent under manager Darrell Johnson. It closed the 1977 season with a 64–98 won-loss record; the 1978 season was even worse, as the team finished 56–104. The seasons from 1979 to 1984 were equally rocky, as the team made four changes in managers, three during midseason.

From 1985 to 1989, the Mariners slowly improved, although they continued to be plagued with management turnover. The Mariners would finally see some dramatically positive changes in 1989, with the arrival of players like Ken Griffey, Jr., who homered off the first pitch thrown to him during his first game in Seattle and, of course, Randy Johnson.

When Johnson arrived in Seattle, manager Jim Lefebvre told him, "You're going to pitch every five days." The team was planning to use its newest acquisition as much as possible, which was just fine with Johnson.

In his first game for Seattle, against the New York Yankees on May 30, 1989, Johnson was nervous. The Yankee fans were not friendly: As he stood on the mound, Johnson heard jeers from the crowd. "From all corners of the ballpark, Johnson heard every possible unkind comment about his height and appearance," Matt Christopher writes. He responded by striking out the first batter, the formidable Rickey Henderson. In fact, Johnson pitched the first six innings well, and the Mariners defeated the team popularly known as the Bronx Bombers, 3-2, with Johnson getting the win. Biographer Larry Stone adds that Griffey contributed two home runs to that effort, and explains, "No one knew it yet, but Randy and Ken would become the most productive players in Mariner history."

Randy Johnson is pictured in action during a game in 1990, his second season with the Seattle Mariners. In June 1990, Johnson pitched a no-hitter against the Detroit Tigers—the first in Mariners history. The win in that game was only the fourteenth of Johnson's career.

Despite an excellent beginning, Johnson finished his first season as a Mariner with a 7–9 record and a 4.40 ERA. He walked 70 batters. His problems with control continued to

☆ ☆ ☆ ☆ ☆
THE NO-HITTER

During the 1990 season, Randy Johnson wanted to figure out a way to give up fewer home runs. So he sat down with catcher Scott Bradley to discuss pitching strategy before the Mariners played the Detroit Tigers on June 2. They decided that Johnson should concentrate on throwing his fastball inside to batters because it was difficult to make solid contact on those types of pitches, especially when they were close to 100 miles per hour (161 kilometers per hour).

The plan worked better than Johnson and Bradley could have imagined. Not only did Johnson not allow any homers, he did not give up any hits as the Mariners beat the Tigers, 2-0. It was Johnson's first no-hitter, the first ever by a Mariners pitcher, and the first thrown at the Seattle Kingdome, which opened for baseball in 1977.

The no-hitter did not come easily for Johnson, though. The Big Unit had to overcome control problems throughout the game. He struck out eight batters, but he walked six and had to pitch out of a big jam in the sixth inning.

Johnson walked Tony Phillips with one out and Gary Ward walked one out later to put two runners on base for Cecil Fielder. The slugger came into the game tied for first place in the major leagues with 19 home runs, and Johnson had already allowed 12 homers, the most in the majors at that point. Johnson walked Fielder to load the bases, but the left-hander struck out Chet Lemon to escape trouble and end the sixth inning.

haunt him, and he knew he still had many improvements to make. Johnson began to work harder than ever in the off-season.

☆ ☆ ☆ ☆ ☆

The Tigers almost got a hit the next inning when Tracy Jones hit a slow grounder to third base. Edgar Martinez scooped it up, but his throw pulled first baseman Alvin Davis off the bag. Umpire Derryl Cousins ruled that Davis tagged Jones on the helmet, preventing the scorekeeper from having to make a tough decision on whether to give Jones a hit or charge Martinez with a throwing error. Tigers manager Sparky Anderson came out of the dugout to argue the call, but he said after the game that Jones told him he was out.

The hardest-hit ball all night came off Ward's bat in the first inning. Ward hit a fly ball that center fielder Ken Griffey, Jr., caught just in front of the warning track.

With 20,014 fans on their feet in anticipation of every pitch in the ninth inning, Johnson struck out Fielder on three pitches for the first out. Lemon fouled out to Davis for the second out, bringing catcher Mike Heath to the plate. Heath was no easy out. He entered the game with a .360 batting average, though he grounded out twice and struck out his first three times up in this game.

Johnson quickly got two strikes on Heath, then blew a 98-mile-per-hour (158-kilometer-per-hour) fastball past him for the final out. The crowd roared as Johnson celebrated on the mound with his teammates. Overall, Johnson threw 136 pitches, including 87 strikes and 49 balls. The Mariners said he had 50 pitches of 94 miles per hour (151 kilometers per hour) or more. The victory was the fourteenth in Johnson's career and his first shutout.

Off the field, Johnson's personal life was also becoming complicated. Johnson had been dating Laurel Roszell, a young woman who soon became pregnant with his child. The couple broke up during the pregnancy, however. Heather Roszell was born in September 1989. Johnson agreed to support her and a few years later began to make child-support payments to his former girlfriend, who was in charge of the child's upbringing.

Before Heather was born, Johnson attended a charity golf event and met a young woman named Lisa. She was six feet tall and very pleasant. The two eventually began to date, and their relationship became more and more serious.

Just as promising was Johnson's effort in a game two months into the new season. On June 2, 1990, he made headlines in Seattle—and nationally. Johnson threw the first no-hitter in the history of the Seattle Mariners. His last pitch, which struck out Mike Heath, was clocked at 98 miles per hour (158 kilometers per hour). He tossed 136 pitches, striking out eight batters and allowing six walks, against the Detroit Tigers. The Mariners won, 2-0.

"I'm exhausted," Johnson said after the game, "but ecstatic I was able to do something like this." When he was named to the roster for the All-Star Game a few weeks later, Johnson was thrilled. Although he did not get a chance to play in the game, the honor was exciting for him. It meant that he had been recognized as one of baseball's great players.

5

Getting Better

Randy Johnson's pitching style often throws off his opponents. Because his arms are so long, his pitches look like sidearm pitches. While the batter waits for the ball to arrive at the plate, the ball appears as if it is zooming toward the batter from the side. The angle, combined with the amazing speed and power of the pitch, completely baffles most batters. Also, because his legs are so long, Johnson lands farther in front of the pitching rubber than most pitchers. Teammate Ken Griffey, Jr., once said, "It looked like he was just handing the ball to the catcher."

Johnson's dominant performance in the no-hitter against the Tigers earned him newfound respect in Seattle, a city that had been upset to lose Mark Langston. The no-hitter was also

Randy Johnson's pitching style often confuses batters. His long arms make his delivery appear to be sidearmed. Combine the angle with Johnson's power, and most batters are stymied.

an illustration that he was finally learning, slowly but surely, to rein in his formerly uncontrollable left arm.

He knew, though, that he had a long way to go. "It was a good no-hitter," he said later, "but not a great no-hitter." In fact, his father made certain that the achievement did not make Johnson overly confident in his abilities. "My father really instilled in me to never be satisfied with anything," Johnson told reporter Bob Brookover. "I can remember when I pitched my no-hitter against Detroit in 1990. I called my dad from the clubhouse and told him about it. He asked me how many walks I had."

Focusing on the areas in which he needed improvement helped prevent Johnson from developing an inflated ego. He continued to work on polishing and honing his skills.

During his early years with the Mariners, Johnson also developed his professional personality along with his playing skills. With his long, mullet hairstyle and tall, lanky figure, he became a sight that was difficult for baseball fans in Seattle to miss. He also cultivated a habit of staring down batters with an unblinking, intimidating look that unnerved many of them.

Others knew that Johnson had a much softer, more playful side than the one he presented to opponents on the mound. When he first arrived in Seattle, for example, he earned a reputation among his new teammates as a jokester: "The first thing Johnson did was surround his locker with bright yellow police-barricade tape," Christopher writes. He also pulled a few pranks on the fans. "One favorite was to throw baseballs attached to long strips of adhesive tape to fans in the stands, then pull them back out of reach."

In 1991, thanks to the hitting and fielding skills of Ken Griffey, Jr., and the dominant pitching arm of Johnson, the Mariners recorded their best season ever, 83 wins and 79 losses.

One of the most exciting games was a shutout that Johnson pitched against the Oakland Athletics. A shutout is a game in which the opposing team does not score any runs. Johnson pitched the entire game and even had a no-hitter until the final inning, when he allowed one batter to get a hit and get on base. He rallied to finish the inning and preserve the Mariners' 4-0 victory.

Johnson's record for the 1991 season, 13–10, was still not stellar, but it was a sign of improvement. (Johnson actually gave up more walks—152—than hits—151—indicating his continued lack of total control over his pitches.) Johnson was developing his talent right along with that of his ball club.

THE INFLUENCE OF NOLAN RYAN

Johnson started the 1992 season on the wrong foot. His pitches were out of control, and he was walking too many batters. The Mariners' new manager, Bill Plummer, was unhappy with his performance, saying once after a Mariners defeat that Johnson "quit on us and quit on the team."

Indeed, Johnson was not a consistent pitcher. He knew it. He had always known it. The problem was that he did not know how to improve. His occasional wildness made him very nervous. His family and his teammates knew not to get too close to him on days when he was starting a game, because he was like a live wire. He often spent the days when he was starting a game by relaxing as well as he could, such as by playing the drums to loosen his nerves. He never could predict, though, if he would have a good night or a bad one.

Little did he know that help was on the way.

In the middle of the season, the Mariners went to Texas to play the Rangers, and there, Johnson met pitching legend Nolan Ryan. Johnson had one session with Ryan, and it potentially influenced his entire pitching career.

Ryan, who played for 27 seasons, would be elected to the Baseball Hall of Fame in 1999. Like Randy Johnson, though, he understood how it felt to struggle early in his career.

Born in 1947 in Texas, Ryan began his major-league career playing for the New York Mets in 1965. He joined the California Angels in 1972, the Houston Astros in 1980, and the Texas Rangers in 1989. Ryan was a record-setting pitcher whom most young hurlers, like Johnson, admired. In 1983, Ryan broke Walter Johnson's record of 3,508 career strikeouts, which had been set in 1927. When Ryan retired 10 years later, he had 5,714 strikeouts to his credit. He played professional baseball until he was 46 years old, much later than most players, especially pitchers.

In 1992, Ryan was approaching the end of his career. He had decided to work with pitching coach Tom House on a video entitled *Fastball,* which was intended to teach pitching techniques to young pitchers. Ryan and House wanted to include Johnson, one of the big names in pitching, on the video. Johnson, who had a tremendous amount of respect for Ryan, happily agreed. It was not every day that one of pitching's greatest legends offered a young player free advice.

And Johnson felt he needed it, according to Matt Christopher: "Johnson had worked hard over the years and had made some improvements, but he was still mystified by the way his control would suddenly desert him for no reason."

As Ryan watched Johnson pitch, he mentioned an important fact to him. Ryan suggested that Johnson land on the ball of his foot, rather than just on the heel of his foot when he strode toward home plate. When Johnson landed on his heel, his leg was not able—as it should have been—to absorb the full impact of his foot; instead the impact reverberated in his upper body. The awkward landing caused his arm to drop slightly, which made his pitches inconsistent.

Landing on the ball of his foot would allow his whole foot to take the impact and would leave his arms free and uninhibited. He would have more control over his pitches, because his landing would be more stable and Johnson would be more in line with home plate.

In 1992, his twenty-sixth season in the major leagues, Nolan Ryan of the Texas Rangers took to the mound in a game against the Chicago White Sox. During that year, Ryan gave Randy Johnson some advice that helped him with his control. He told Johnson to land on the ball of his foot, not the heel, when he strode toward home plate.

Johnson tried the technique, working on it for several days. It made a major difference in his delivery. Suddenly, he was throwing fewer wild pitches; indeed, his pitches were finding home plate with deadly accuracy.

Was it odd that a pitcher from an opposing team would offer some advice to Johnson? It is a testament to Nolan Ryan's geniality and professionalism as a sportsman: He later said that he saw Johnson's talent and wanted to help him perfect his game.

Johnson has never made a secret of the fact that Ryan helped him tremendously. He credits Ryan for changing his career.

THE DEATH OF BUD JOHNSON

In December 1992, Johnson's father suffered an aortic aneurysm. (An aneurysm is a bulge in a blood vessel.) Johnson was on his way home to visit his parents for the holidays, but he could not get there in time to see his father before he died. Rollen "Bud" Johnson passed away on December 25, Christmas Day.

The Johnson family was devastated. Johnson struggled for a way to cope with the loss of the man who was his role model. "After he passed away," Johnson said, "I seriously thought about giving baseball up. I enjoyed the thrill of telling my dad how good I was on a given night. When he passed away, I realized I had no one to call."

Bud Johnson had been a guide to his children on how to live. "I learned how to push myself when he was alive," Johnson later told reporter Bob Brookover. "He was the disciplinarian in our house, and he instilled discipline in me. He taught me that a lot of times in life you only have the opportunity to do something once and you better do it right the first time."

Increasingly, Johnson turned to religion to cope with his father's death and to accept it. He became a born-again Christian in early 1993. As a symbol of his newly recharged faith, he drew a cross and wrote his father's name on the inside of his baseball glove. Around this time he became committed to his girlfriend, Lisa, and they married in 1993. Lisa agreed with Randy's desire to live a Christian lifestyle.

Johnson also became involved with charitable associations, especially those that benefited the homeless and children. He once said, "Nolan Ryan helped me with baseball, and my dad passing away gave me a bigger heart."

Many people also saw more positive changes in Johnson's pitching during this period. He became more serious and focused on his playing skills, and his performance showed it. The 1993 baseball season was a good one for him and for the Mariners.

The ball club had a new manager (yet again). After the Mariners finished in last place in their division in 1992, the team's owner knew that more change was needed. Lou Piniella, one of baseball's most fiery managers, was hired.

★ ★ ★ ★ ★ ☆

RANDY JOHNSON VS. JOHN KRUK

The fastball slipped out of Randy Johnson's hand at the 1993 All-Star Game and sailed way over John Kruk's head. Kruk jumped out of the batter's box, took his helmet off, and smiled.

Kruk was relieved that the pitch did not hit him, but he was not too eager to see another one like it. Like many other batters, Kruk feared the Big Unit. Unlike most players, Kruk did not hide his feelings.

A burly left-handed hitter with a pear-shaped body, Kruk paced around before he timidly stepped back into the batter's box. He patted his heart, shook his head, and fanned himself. Kruk got a comforting tap from catcher Iván Rodríguez, took a deep breath, and got ready for Johnson's next pitch.

Kruk did not want to take any chances this time, so he bailed out before Johnson's fastball caught the inside corner for the first strike.

Players in both dugouts roared in laughter while the announcers laughed and tried to explain Kruk's actions. "He wants no part of Randy Johnson. None. Nada," broadcaster Tim McCarver said.

Johnson's next pitch was a breaking ball. Kruk swung wildly and missed, spinning completely around in the box. "It looks like a rope was on his right leg," McCarver said.

Johnson reared back and fired a fastball. Kruk took another wild swing and missed again. Strike three. Inning over.

Happy that he survived his at-bat and totally unfazed by striking out, Kruk bent over as if he were bowing at Johnson, flipped

Piniella had been a terrific ballplayer, one who could really swing a bat. He had played for the Cleveland Indians, the Baltimore Orioles, the Kansas City Royals, and the New York Yankees. In the late 1980s, he started his managing career with

☆ ☆ ☆ ☆ ☆

his helmet off, and flashed a wide grin. Johnson winked at Kruk as he walked off the mound, and the two stars shared a soda in the clubhouse after they both left the game.

The All-Star Game has provided plenty of memorable moments over the years. Perhaps none were more comical than Kruk's at-bat against Johnson in the 1993 Midsummer Classic in Baltimore.

Kruk played first base for the Philadelphia Phillies and was one of the best hitters on a team that was in first place in the National League East. His batting average at the All-Star break was .350, but that did not matter against Johnson. The hard-throwing left-hander was playing in his second All-Star Game, and opposing players were starting to realize just how scary it was to face him.

It took just one pitch to intimidate Kruk. He was terrified once Johnson's 98-mile-per-hour (158-kilometer-per-hour) fastball flew over him to the backstop. "He's going to kill somebody," Kruk said later.

The situation amused Johnson. "It was a bit humid out there, and I think the ball just got away, but John has the type of personality, I think, that he didn't think anything of it and he got a little reaction out of it," Johnson told reporters.

Kruk finished the game 0-for-3. Johnson retired all six batters he faced. The American League beat the National League, 9-3.

Joking around, Randy Johnson and his wife, Lisa, held out license plates featuring Johnson's nickname at their home in Bellevue, Washington. After dating for four years, the couple married in 1993.

the Yankees. He then managed the Cincinnati Reds for a couple of years, leading the team to a World Series victory in 1990. In 1993, he joined the Mariners as a manager, and he would become one of the team's most influential directors.

Known for his hot temper, Piniella was frequently ejected from games for arguing with the umpires. Piniella wanted things done his way and done right. If pitchers did not pitch well, he removed them from the game. He was, nevertheless, generally patient with his players, but he expected them to work hard.

He provided stability to a team that needed it. His players began to play more cohesively. In 1995, he was named the

American League Manager of the Year. The Mariners began to rack up the wins, and in 2001, they tied a record set by the Chicago Cubs in 1906 with 116 victories. Coming from a team that had recorded more than 100 losses three times in franchise history, the improvement was remarkable.

6

A New and Improved Randy Johnson

Randy Johnson was ready to play and play hard. In a game against the Oakland Athletics on May 16, 1993, he almost had a perfect game, which is when nobody gets on base, whether with a walk, a hit, or an error. In the eighth inning, Johnson walked one batter, who was called out on a double play. He walked two more and gave up a single in the ninth inning, but for more than seven innings, he pitched a perfect game. The Mariners won, 7-0, and everybody paid attention to the new Randy Johnson.

This was a Randy Johnson with power and control—he could throw a ball exactly where he wanted, and he could throw it hard. Even the A's manager, Tony La Russa, admitted that his team never had a chance that day against Johnson.

Johnson, however, gave credit to someone else for his amazing performance. After the last strikeout, he threw up his arms in excitement. Then he looked up to the sky and put his gloved hand to his heart. "I felt my father's presence," he said later. "When I pointed up afterwards, it was for my dad. If I have a guardian angel, it's my father."

He finished the 1993 season with a 19–8 record, an impressive ERA of 3.24, and 308 strikeouts. His strikeout total led the American League for the second year in a row. The Mariners signed a new four-year contract with him for $20.25 million. His new style and ability to control his pitches made him a much more valuable player.

He continued his prowess on the mound in 1994, compiling a 13–6 record, with a 3.19 ERA and 294 strikeouts, before a players' strike halted the season on August 12. The labor problems involved the desire by team owners to put a salary cap in place as a way to keep costs down. The players opposed a salary cap. When negotiations failed to reach a compromise, the players decided to go on strike. The walkout led to the cancellation of the World Series in 1994. The strike continued into 1995 until the players decided in early April to return to the field without a new labor agreement. During that long stretch of time off, on December 28, 1994, Lisa Johnson gave birth to Samantha, the couple's first child together.

Though the 1995 season started late, Johnson was in good shape, and he had one of his best seasons ever. He finished the year with an 18–2 record, a 2.48 ERA, and 294 strikeouts. That year, he was thrilled to be the winner of the Cy Young Award in the American League. The Cy Young Award, which is voted on by members of the Baseball Writers' Association of America, is the most prestigious honor for pitchers in baseball.

Cy Young's real name was Denton True Young, but his nickname was "Cyclone." He began his major-league career in 1890

The Seattle Mariners and Randy Johnson both had great years in 1995. Johnson, who had an 18–2 record, won his first Cy Young Award that season. And Seattle was able to reach postseason play. Here, Johnson pitches in Game 6 of the American League Championship Series against the Cleveland Indians. The Indians won the series, though, to end Seattle's season.

and quickly set records with a fastball that became legendary. His stamina was also well-known; in those days, pitchers were expected to pitch the entire game, as no relief pitchers were used. In 1956, a year after Young's death, baseball commissioner Ford Frick began to give out the prize to recognize the best pitcher of the year. Later, the practice became to honor the best pitcher in each league.

Johnson was an excellent choice for the 1995 Cy Young Award; that year, he helped the Mariners finish first in the

American League West with a record of 79–66. Seattle had come back from 13 games out of first place in August to catch the California Angels on the final day. The team then won a one-game playoff to advance to the postseason. In the first round of the playoffs, the Mariners beat the Yankees. The team advanced to the American League Championship Series but lost to the Cleveland Indians, four games to two.

Nonetheless, Seattle baseball fans commonly refer to the 1995 season as the "Miracle Season." The motto "refuse to lose" could regularly be heard as the Mariners advanced into the postseason. The team's amazing run revived interest in baseball among Seattle's fans and helped to make Johnson a more recognized baseball personality.

THE DISABLED LIST

Randy and Lisa Johnson's son, Tanner, was born on April 5, 1996—it seemed like a good omen for the beginning of a new baseball season. In fact, Johnson started out the year 5–0. The 1996 season, however, would become one fraught with problems, mostly because of a back injury.

It started on April 26, when Johnson left a game during the fourth inning because his back—which had been sore during spring training—began to hurt him terribly. "When I landed on my front foot, it was like a knife being jabbed in my back," he recalls in *Randy Johnson: Arizona Heat!* After his back continued to bother him, he finally had it examined. The diagnosis was a bulging disc in his spine.

Spinal discs are like shock absorbers that help protect the spine. They also act as connectors between the vertebrae, allowing the spine to bend and move. The bulging disc in Johnson's spine was causing a lot of pain in his back as well as his leg. Johnson found it painful just to walk, much less to pitch. Although people experience problems with spinal discs as they age, it is not surprising that Johnson had such trouble. Because of his height, his back naturally absorbed a lot of the impact when he pitched. The strain had caused, over time, the problems he began to experience so much in 1996.

The Mariners allowed Johnson three months to rest, hoping the time off would be effective in easing his pain and allowing the disc to heal. When he returned to the mound, though, he continued to have pain and difficulty, so he was put back on the disabled list. This time, the problem was diagnosed as a herniated disc, which means that the disc was pressing on the nerves of his backbone. In September, he underwent surgery to remove a part of the disc.

Johnson spent most of the fall and winter rehabilitating his back. He was very anxious, and the media scrutiny—including some skepticism about the future of his career—began to play on his nerves. He described that period as "an emotional roller-coaster."

"I don't want to take that ride again," he said in *Randy Johnson: Arizona Heat!* "No one knew what was really happening, that I tried to compete through the pain last year, that I'd come in between innings and lie with my legs raised to relieve the pain." He also admitted that being upset about his injury caused tension in his marriage. Lisa Johnson, though, understood what he was enduring, and she supported him emotionally throughout the ordeal.

COMING BACK

Johnson took his time recovering from the spinal surgery. He eased himself slowly into a strengthening routine, and he was surprised to discover that even the most mundane, everyday activities tested his abilities. He was determined, however, to return to baseball during the 1997 season.

He did return, more dominant than ever. Any question about the effect of his back injury on his pitching ability was wiped out during this season. He had a 20–4 record—posting 20 wins in a regular season is a major achievement for any pitcher—and a 2.28 ERA. He also was second in the American

(*continues on page 54*)

Randy Johnson saluted the crowd at the Kingdome as he left the field after the ninth inning of a game on June 24, 1997, against the Athletics. Johnson struck out 19 Oakland batters, but Seattle still lost, 4-1. Mark McGwire of the A's hit a monster home run off Johnson in the game.

☆ ☆ ☆ ☆ ☆ ☆

JOHNSON STRIKES OUT 19 BUT LOSES

Randy Johnson threw so hard that sometimes when a hitter made solid contact, the ball traveled a long, long way. Mark McGwire hit plenty of home runs in his major-league career—583, to be exact.

Every time Johnson faced his former college teammate, it was a classic battle: power versus power.

On June 24, 1997, Johnson was pitching for the Seattle Mariners against the Oakland Athletics. Johnson's fastball was blazing that night, but McGwire caught up to it in the fifth inning. The A's slugger hit a 97-mile-per-hour (156-kilometer-per-hour) fastball 538 feet (164 meters) into the second deck in left field at Seattle's Kingdome.

"When we were teammates at Southern California, I saw him hit a lot of long home runs," Johnson said in Associated Press sportswriter Jim Cour's article. "But they were with an aluminum bat. Tonight, I never saw a person hit a ball that far. I wasn't really sure if I should go up to home plate and con-gratulate him."

McGwire's blast amazed Johnson, but the Big Unit left plenty of hitters and spectators in awe that night. Johnson ended up striking out 19 batters to break the American League record for a left-handed pitcher. He even fanned McGwire twice. Mark Bellhorn struck out four times, and Jose Canseco, Jason McDonald, and Patrick Lennon went down three times each.

Remarkably, the A's got 11 hits off Johnson and won 4-1. The 19 strikeouts by Johnson were one short of the major-league record for a nine-inning game set by Roger Clemens. Ron Guidry

☆ ☆ ☆ ☆ ☆ ☆

of the New York Yankees previously held the American League record for lefties with 18 strikeouts against California on June 17, 1978.

As Cour reported, McGwire said: "When you're facing Randy, he has a curveball that starts at Everett (30 miles north of Seattle) and finishes here at the Kingdome. Plus a 100-mile-per-hour fastball. You look for a pitch or a location and hopefully you get it. If you don't, you're in trouble."

McGwire's strategy against Johnson was simple. "You just pray to the God upstairs," McGwire said in Cour's article.

Johnson struck out 15 batters in the first six innings but fanned no one in the seventh. He added three more victims in the eighth and had a chance to break the record with three more in the ninth.

Johnson had thrown 127 pitches through eight innings. Mariners manager Lou Piniella had limited Johnson to a maximum of 130 pitches since he had returned from back surgery, but he allowed his pitcher to surpass that amount because he had a chance to break Clemens's record.

In the ninth, Johnson got two strikes on Scott Brosius before he hit a fly ball for the first out. George Williams followed with a home run, but Johnson struck out rookie Mark Bellhorn for No. 19. Needing one more strikeout to tie Clemens, Johnson got his last out on a fly ball by rookie Jason McDonald.

While he was happy to get all the strikeouts, Johnson was disappointed that he lost the game. "I'm human, and I made some bad pitches," Johnson told Cour. "But it was an exciting game. It was exciting to me."

(*continued from page 50*)

League in strikeouts, one behind league leader Roger Clemens. Johnson's total of 291 gave him an average of 12.3 strikeouts per nine innings. In two separate games that season, he recorded 19 strikeouts.

He still threw wild pitches, however, at least occasionally. In one March spring training game against the San Francisco Giants, he threw a hard pitch to first baseman J. T. Snow. The ball hit Snow in the wrist and bounced up into his face, slamming him in the eye. Later, a CT scan showed that Snow's left eye socket had been fractured. The Giant player was temporarily sidelined until the fracture healed and his vision, which was blurred, returned to normal.

The Mariners won the American League West again in 1997, but they failed to advance in the American League Division Series, defeated by the Baltimore Orioles three games to one.

During the off-season and into 1998, when Johnson should have been looking forward to another solid year, he began to grow unhappy as a Mariner. He was going to become a free agent at the end of the season—free to sign a contract with any team he wished. Johnson hoped to get a contract extension with Seattle before then. The ball club, however, had a tight budget; it did not offer him an extension and announced that the Mariners would entertain trade offers for the pitcher. Johnson was upset because he felt that the team should do more to keep him on its roster, especially after he had such a solid season in 1997.

As usual, Johnson allowed his emotions to interfere with his play. He was an intense player, and everyone—from his parents, to his high school and college coaches, to his big-league managers—had always warned him about letting his frustrations affect his performance. Perhaps anxiety about his future with the Mariners led him to a 9–10 record in the first half of the year, with an ERA of 4.33, an abysmal performance for a pitcher with his demonstrated talent.

In the middle of a game on July 31, 1998, Lou Piniella, the manager of the Seattle Mariners, leaned down to tell Randy Johnson he had just been traded to the Houston Astros. "I feel a little betrayed," Johnson said after the game about the Mariners' actions.

His daughter Willow was born on April 23 of that year, which was perhaps the sole highlight. In July Johnson was suddenly traded to the Houston Astros of the National League for pitchers Freddy García and John Halama and shortstop Carlos

Guillén. The trade was made just a few hours before the trading deadline for the season.

The news stunned Seattle fans. It also upset Johnson. "I would have loved to have been a Mariner forever," he said, "and finished my career there. I feel bad for a lot of people. The Seattle fans. My teammates in Seattle. My family and myself."

He was also upset at how the trade happened. He had been at a game on the night of the trade, sitting in the dugout while the Mariners played the Yankees. After the 9 P.M. deadline passed, his manager, Lou Piniella, told him about the trade.

"I feel a little betrayed," he told the media. "I feel like I've given my best years to date to the Mariners. I helped them save baseball in Seattle."

MOVING TO HOUSTON

When he donned the Astros uniform, Johnson immediately won the respect of the Houston fans. In his first start against the Pittsburgh Pirates, he won the game and had 12 strikeouts. He also pitched four straight shutouts in front of the Houston fans in his first four home games. He finished the season with a 10–1 record and a 1.28 ERA, giving him an overall 19–11 record for the 1998 season. The Astros finished first in the National League Central but lost in the first round of the play-offs to the San Diego Padres. Nevertheless, the Big Unit had had an excellent second half of the season.

Gerry Hunsicker, the Astros' general manager, had been very intent on bringing Johnson to Houston. He said of his star pitcher, "He's exceeded all our expectations." The Astro fans felt the same way; Johnson had quickly become a hero in Houston.

At the end of the season, Johnson became a free agent. Houston surely would want to keep him. Other teams would love to have him. Sports commentators and journalists buzzed about the big question: Where would the Big Unit go next?

To the Diamondbacks

Teams lined up to pursue Randy Johnson when the Big Unit became a free agent after the 1998 season.

General managers for the Anaheim Angels, the Los Angeles Dodgers, and the Texas Rangers got their checkbooks ready and were eager to spend the millions it would take to bring the most dominant left-handed pitcher in baseball to their team.

Of course, the Houston Astros wanted to retain Johnson, who helped them reach the playoffs that season by going 10–1 with a 1.28 ERA after he was acquired in a trade with Seattle.

And, the New York Yankees always seemed to have an interest in every big-name player available because they had an endless flow of revenue and could afford just about anyone's contract. So when Johnson agreed to a four-year deal for $52.4 million with the Arizona Diamondbacks on November 30, 1998, it came as a huge surprise to baseball insiders and fans.

Many questioned Johnson's desire to win a championship. Why would anyone want to play for a team that was in just its second year of existence?

The Diamondbacks won 65 games, lost 97, and finished last in the National League West in their first season as an expansion club. Critics said that Johnson simply went for the money. Johnson considered many factors, however, including the fact that he already had a home in Paradise Valley, a swanky suburb of Phoenix. He also thought that the Diamondbacks were making a strong commitment to building a winner.

The team signed pitchers Todd Stottlemyre and Armando Reynoso a week earlier, bolstering the starting rotation. The addition of Johnson gave the young Diamondbacks an experienced pitching staff that would help the team become an immediate contender.

"We tried to weigh all the factors—how competitive the team would be in the future, where his family would be comfortable," Johnson's agent, Barry Meister, said in an article written by Ronald Blum for The Associated Press. "Money was a non-factor because everything was pretty comparable. He made the decision late, late, late last night, slept on it, still felt that way in the morning, and we called the other clubs."

The naysayers were not only criticizing Johnson; they were also taking shots at Jerry Colangelo, the Diamondbacks' managing general partner, for taking such a financial risk on a pitcher considered past his prime at the age of 35.

With an average salary of $13.1 million per season, the contract made Johnson the second-highest-paid player in the major leagues behind Mo Vaughn, who agreed a week earlier to a six-year, $80 million contract with Anaheim that averaged $13.3 million a season.

In an article by Associated Press writer Bob Baum, Colangelo said:

The marketplace dictates what you need to do, and the fact is that was what the market was for Randy. To play the game, you have to accept the risk. And this is not a blind risk. He is that dominant to where you would be prepared to take that risk with him more than with someone else. Randy Johnson is one of those fierce competitors. He comes to play. When he has his game face on, when he's out there ready to roll, you've got a chance for anything to happen, including a no-hitter or 20 strikeouts, an unbelievable performance. You know you're going to be in every game.

SILENCING THE DOUBTERS

Johnson silenced the critics with an outstanding season in 1999. He went 17–9 with a 2.48 ERA, and he led the majors in strikeouts (364), complete games (12), and innings pitched (271 2/3). He had 10 or more strikeouts in 23 games, tying Nolan Ryan's major-league record for most in a season and breaking Sandy Koufax's National League record set in 1964.

These superior statistics helped Johnson earn his second Cy Young Award, and he joined Gaylord Perry and Pedro Martínez as the only pitchers to win the honor in each league. More important, Johnson was a major reason the Diamondbacks won 100 games, finished in first place, and became the first team in major-league history to reach the playoffs in just their second year of competition.

Johnson, though, pitched poorly in his only playoff start. He gave up seven earned runs in 8 1/3 innings in Game 1 of the National League Division Series against the New York Mets. Johnson left the game with the bases loaded and the score tied at 4-4 in the ninth inning, but Edgardo Alfonzo hit a grand slam off reliever Bobby Chouinard to lead the Mets to an 8-4 win.

Arizona lost the series in four games to the Mets. Still, the season was considered a tremendous success for the Diamondbacks, who defied the odds by going from worst to first in their division in only one year.

Randy Johnson received congratulations from Hanley Frias *(right)* after the Diamondbacks beat the San Francisco Giants on September 24, 1999, to win the National League West. Surrounding them were teammates Kelly Stinnett *(left)*, Matt Williams *(in back)*, and Erubiel Durazo. The Diamondbacks were going to the playoffs in only their second year in existence.

The next season did not go as well for the Diamondbacks, although Johnson won his second straight Cy Young Award after going 19–7 with a 2.64 ERA. Arizona finished in third place with 85 wins despite acquiring another star pitcher, Curt Schilling, from the Philadelphia Phillies midway through the season.

Johnson tied a modern-day record with six victories in April and led the league in strikeouts (347). He recorded his 3,000th strikeout on September 10, as he whiffed Florida Marlins third baseman Mike Lowell.

REWRITING HISTORY

Johnson continued his dominance in 2001. Just one month into the season, on May 8, he recorded 20 strikeouts in nine innings against the Cincinnati Reds. Johnson left the game after the ninth inning with the score still tied. Because the game went 11 innings, he initially did not get credit for sharing the major-league record for strikeouts in a nine-inning game with Roger Clemens and Kerry Wood. Major League Baseball, however, reversed the ruling a month later and allowed Johnson's game to enter the record book.

Johnson was not done rewriting history. On July 19 against the San Diego Padres, he came out of the bullpen and struck out 16 batters in seven innings to break Walter Johnson's 88-year-old record for most strikeouts in a relief appearance.

Johnson pitched in relief that day because the game was suspended the previous night after two innings when two electrical explosions knocked out a light tower in Qualcomm Stadium in San Diego. When the game resumed the following day, Johnson replaced Schilling, the starter, in the top of the third inning.

Johnson again was the starting pitcher for the National League in the All-Star Game on July 10 (he had also been the starter in the 1995, 1997, and 2000 games). The All-Star Game gave him a chance to return to Seattle and pitch in the city where he first achieved his fame. It was his eighth trip to the Midsummer Classic, and he pitched two scoreless innings, allowing just one hit.

☆ ☆ ☆ ☆ ☆ ☆

A RECORD THAT ALMOST WASN'T

Only three pitchers in major-league history have struck out 20 batters in nine innings. And one of those players almost did not get his name in the record book.

On May 8, 2001, Randy Johnson was pitching for the Arizona Diamondbacks when he fanned 20 Cincinnati Reds batters to join Roger Clemens and Kerry Wood as the only pitchers to strike out that many batters in nine innings.

The only problem for Johnson was that the Diamondbacks and Reds were tied, 1-1, when he left the game after nine innings. The game went on to last 11 innings. So, the Elias Sports Bureau, baseball's official record keeper, did not list the Big Unit as the co-holder of the record for most strikeouts in a nine-inning game.

Less than a month later, however, Major League Baseball reversed the ruling and allowed Johnson's achievement to enter the record book.

As Mel Reisner reported in his article for The Associated Press, Johnson considered himself tied with Clemens and Wood all along. "I think I do, so when someone says I don't, well I did what they did in nine," Johnson said after the game. "I'm not losing sleep over it. I know what I did. I'm not making a big deal out of it. There are only two other players in the history of baseball who have done it. There's a great deal of satisfaction in doing it."

Mark Grace played first base behind Wood and Johnson in their 20-strikeout games. In Reisner's article, Grace disagreed with Elias's stance. "Anybody who knows baseball realizes he did

On August 23 against Pittsburgh, Johnson fanned Jack Wilson in the first inning for his 1,000th strikeout with the Diamondbacks in less than three seasons. He later whiffed

☆ ☆ ☆ ☆ ☆

the same exact thing that the other guys did, and it was a fabulous accomplishment," Grace said.

Johnson struck out the side in the fourth, seventh, and eighth innings, and fanned two batters in the first, second, third, fifth and ninth innings. He struck out one in the sixth.

Needing two strikeouts to reach 20, Johnson fanned pinch hitter Deion Sanders on three pitches leading off the ninth. After Donnie Sadler grounded out, Johnson blew a pitch past Juan Castro to reach 20 strikeouts.

Realizing he finally reached that magic number after twice getting 19 strikeouts in a game, the normally low-key Johnson celebrated his accomplishment. He threw his right arm in the air, shouted to the sky, and tipped his cap to the cheering crowd as he walked off the field.

A "K" was put on the scoreboard at Bank One Ballpark for each strikeout, but the board ran out of room before Johnson reached 20. Additional K's were then tacked on the side of the board, with lights forming "20" in the middle.

Johnson threw 124 pitches, 92 for strikes. He declined to stay in the game when manager Bob Brenly gave him the opportunity to pitch the tenth inning. Arizona eventually won, 4-3.

"I saw no point in going out there for the tenth inning," Johnson said in Reisner's article. "I surely could have went out there and done it, but what was the point in going out there and throwing 10 innings? I really didn't see it. The outcome is what's important."

The crowd at Bank One Ballpark in Phoenix, Arizona, gave Randy Johnson a standing ovation as he left the field after the ninth inning of a game on May 8, 2001, against the Cincinnati Reds. He struck out 20 batters during the nine innings he pitched—tying the major-league record. The Diamondbacks went on to win the game in 11 innings.

Wilson in the sixth inning for his 300th strikeout of the season, becoming the first pitcher in major-league history to reach 300 strikeouts in four consecutive seasons.

Johnson again tied his and Ryan's record for the most games with double-digit strikeouts in a season when he notched his twenty-third such performance of the year on September 27 against the Milwaukee Brewers. He earned his 200th career win on October 2, pitching seven innings and giving up one run against the Colorado Rockies.

That game was Johnson's final outing of the regular season. He finished the year 21–6 with a 2.49 ERA, led the league with 372 strikeouts, and captured his third straight Cy Young Award. Johnson's strikeouts-per-nine-innings ratio of 13.4 was the best in major-league history, breaking Pedro Martínez's mark of 13.2 in 1999.

The Diamondbacks clinched the National League West championship on October 5, earning their second trip to the playoffs in only their fourth season. Now it was time for Johnson to break his reputation as a pitcher who choked under playoff pressure.

8

The
World Series

Randy Johnson's first chance to overcome his playoff reputation came in the National League Division Series against the St. Louis Cardinals. Johnson pitched well in Game 2, allowing only three runs and six hits and striking out nine in eight innings. Unfortunately, Arizona's hitters did not give him much support. The Cardinals won the game, 4-1, extending Johnson's postseason losing streak to a major-league record seven in a row.

The Diamondbacks eventually won the division series, three games to two, and they advanced to play the Atlanta Braves for the National League pennant, giving Johnson another chance to end the losing skid. Johnson made sure that he did not need much support from the offense in Game 1 against Atlanta. He tossed a complete game, a three-hit

Randy Johnson delivered a pitch in the first inning of Game 1 of the 2001 National League Championship Series in Phoenix against the Atlanta Braves. During one stretch of the game, Johnson retired 20 straight batters in leading Arizona to a 2-0 win. The victory snapped a seven-game postseason losing streak for Johnson.

shutout with 11 strikeouts in the Diamondbacks' 2-0 victory over the Braves.

"We all know what Randy is capable of on a given day, and this was one of those given days," Arizona manager Bob Brenly said in an article by Bob Baum for The Associated Press. "He went out there and pitched like the Big Unit we've all come to know and love."

Johnson was only getting started with his postseason brilliance. He pitched seven innings, gave up two runs, and beat

Atlanta in Game 5 as the Diamondbacks clinched the series and advanced to the World Series for the first time in the team's young history.

★ ☆ ☆ ☆ ☆ ☆
FINALLY, JOHNSON ENDS PLAYOFF LOSING STREAK

When Randy Johnson pitched one inning in relief to help the Seattle Mariners beat the New York Yankees in Game 5 of the 1995 American League Division Series, the Big Unit had no clue it would take him six more years to win another playoff game.

In between, Johnson set a major-league record with seven straight losses in postseason games.

He finally ended that streak of futility and buried his reputation as a big-game flop by tossing a three-hit shutout against the Atlanta Braves in Game 1 of the 2001 National League Championship Series.

Johnson struck out 11 batters, walked one, and helped the Diamondbacks win the first game of the series, 2-0. In the process, he outdueled four-time Cy Young Award winner Greg Maddux.

Naturally, Johnson was relieved to earn a win in the playoffs. "Assuming someone might say here, 'Is this a monkey off your back?' This is more like a gorilla. King Kong," Johnson said in an article by Bob Baum for The Associated Press.

Johnson dominated the Braves. At one point, he retired 20 straight batters before walking Bernard Gilkey with one out in the eighth inning. Johnson was one out away from pitching the eighth one-hitter in postseason history when Julio Franco and Chipper Jones singled to put runners at first and third in the ninth inning. Johnson then struck out Brian Jordan to end the game.

Certainly Johnson was thrilled about reaching the World Series for his first time at the age of 38. "I realize how special it is. There's no guarantee you'll ever get to the World Series,"

★ ☆ ☆ ☆ ☆ ☆

"This kind of game is more mentally draining than it is physically draining, because you realize if you make one mistake that could be the ball game," Johnson said in Baum's article. "They had the go-ahead run up in that last inning. It's just nice to walk off the field and celebrate."

Johnson's losing streak was not entirely a result of his pitching poorly. He did not get much run support from the offense on the teams he played for during that stretch. Johnson had a respectable ERA of 3.84 in the seven playoff games he lost plus one game in which he had no decision.

In the 1995 American League Championship Series against Cleveland, Seattle scored two runs for Johnson in 15 innings. In the 1997 American League Division Series, the Mariners scored two runs against Baltimore in 13 innings for Johnson.

The Houston Astros scored one run in Johnson's 14 innings during the 1998 National League Division Series against San Diego. The Diamondbacks scored one run for Johnson in his eight innings in the National League Division Series against St. Louis in 2001.

The only time that Johnson pitched terribly during that postseason losing streak was in the 1999 National League Division Series when he allowed seven earned runs in $8^{1}/_{3}$ innings against the New York Mets. During his losing streak, Johnson's teams scored a total of 10 runs for him in $58^{2}/_{3}$ innings. That is an average of only 1.5 runs per game.

Johnson said in an article by Ben Walker for The Associated Press. "There's only two or three people on our team who have ever been there. I think we want to enjoy the moment, and then realize we have more work to do.

"A lot of people said we were a veteran team that was too old, that we were on the downside." The Diamondbacks' opponent in the World Series would be the legendary New York Yankees. The Bronx Bombers had won three straight championships and had a major-league record 26 titles.

Arizona, though, had Johnson and Schilling, the best one-two pitching tandem in the league and perhaps the best ever. Schilling was terrific in Game 1 of the World Series, and the Diamondbacks won 9-1.

Feeding off Schilling's performance, Johnson dominated the Yankees in Game 2 in his first World Series start. Johnson pitched a complete-game, three-hit shutout, striking out 11 in Arizona's 4-0 win.

As Walker reported for The Associated Press, the Yankees were completely baffled. "This was one of those games where we were just dominated," Yankees star Derek Jeter said in the article. "They're not just pitching well against me. They were pitching well against everyone."

It was the first complete-game shutout in the World Series since Schilling pitched one in 1993 for the Philadelphia Phillies. "He was terrific. He lived up to what he's supposed to be," Yankees manager Joe Torre said in Walker's article. "The axiom has never changed—good pitching stops good hitting. And that's what we've seen."

Johnson struck out seven of the first nine batters he faced and did not allow a hit until Jorge Posada singled to start the fifth inning. His only jam came in the eighth when Shane Spencer and Alfonso Soriano started off the inning with singles. Then Johnson struck out Scott Brosius looking and got pinch hitter Luis Sojo to ground into a double play.

If his effort against the Braves was not enough, this sensational outing certainly proved that the Big Unit was no big-game flop. He helped the Diamondbacks take a 2-0 lead in the best-of-seven series, which shifted to New York for the next three games.

The Yankees refused to give up. Once they returned to Yankee Stadium, they gained the advantage. Backed by a terrific performance from pitcher Roger Clemens in Game 3, the Yankees won 2-1. Schilling came back to pitch with four days' rest in Game 4 and held the Yankees to one run in seven innings. The Diamondbacks scored twice in the top of the eighth to take a 3-1 lead, and closer Byung-Hyun Kim was called upon to finish off New York.

Kim struck out the side in the bottom of the eighth but allowed a two-run homer to Tino Martinez with two outs in the ninth that sent the game into extra innings. Jeter homered off Kim with two outs in the tenth inning to win it for the Yankees and tie the World Series at two games apiece.

Arizona was not deflated by the loss and took another two-run lead in Game 5. Once again, though, Kim blew it for the Diamondbacks. This time, Scott Brosius hit a two-run homer off Kim with two outs in the ninth inning to tie the score at 2-2 and send the game into extra innings. Soriano's run-scoring single in the twelfth inning lifted the Yankees to their second straight dramatic victory and gave New York a three-games-to-two lead.

All the momentum had shifted to the Yankees, and it was up to Johnson to keep the Diamondbacks' championship hopes alive when the World Series returned to Bank One Ballpark in Phoenix for Game 6.

With no margin for error, the Diamondbacks made sure they would not need help from their bullpen. The offense pounded out 22 hits and scored 15 runs to the Yankees' 2 runs, making it an easy night for Johnson. He blanked the Yankees

Randy Johnson had a hand in the offense, too, in Game 6 of the 2001 World Series against the New York Yankees, getting a hit here in the second inning. Johnson scored two runs, for the first time in his career, as the Diamondbacks throttled the Yankees, 15-2, setting up a decisive Game 7.

until the sixth inning, left after the seventh, and kept open the possibility of even pitching in relief in Game 7.

Johnson also joined in the fun on offense, delivering an RBI single in the third inning. He scored two runs for the first time in his career, making him the first pitcher to do so in a World Series game since Bob Gibson in 1968.

"Everybody came out hitting the ball well tonight," Johnson said in an article by Walker for The Associated Press. "Tip your hat to all of our hitters tonight. It makes your job easier."

GAME SEVEN

The final game of the World Series would come down to Schilling vs. Clemens, a classic battle between two of the game's best right-handed pitchers.

Schilling, making his third start in the World Series, pitched well. But Clemens was even better. Soriano led off the top of the eighth inning with a solo home run off Schilling to give New York a 2-1 lead.

Schilling struck out the next batter, but pinch hitter David Justice hit a single. Reliever Miguel Batista replaced Schilling and got Derek Jeter to ground into a fielder's choice. With the left-handed-hitting Paul O'Neill coming up and a runner on first base, Diamondbacks manager Bob Brenly was not taking any more chances. He called in the Big Unit.

Johnson had to be tired after throwing 103 pitches the night before. But the Diamondbacks' relievers had blown two games in the World Series, and they could not afford to lose another one. Besides, Johnson figured he had four months to rest his arm.

Once the Yankees saw that Johnson was coming in, they sent in Chuck Knoblauch, a right-handed hitter. Johnson retired Knoblauch to end the inning and went to the bench, hoping his teammates could rally against Mariano Rivera, one of the best closers in baseball history.

Rivera struck out three of the four batters he faced in the bottom of the eighth to preserve the Yankees' lead. Johnson answered by retiring the side in order in the top of the ninth, striking out Jorge Posada to end the inning. The 38-year-old lefty did his job. He faced four batters and got them all out. All he could do now was sit in the dugout and hope his teammates

Randy Johnson and Curt Schilling were named co-recipients of the 2001 World Series Most Valuable Player award. Here, after Game 7, Johnson showed off the World Series trophy while Schilling held the MVP award. "Me and Curt fed off one another all year long," Johnson said.

fared well against Rivera, who had saved 23 straight games in the postseason.

The stage was set for an improbable comeback.

Mark Grace singled to start the ninth inning, and Rivera unraveled. David Dellucci was sent in as a pinch runner for Grace, and Damian Miller tried to bunt him over to second base. An error by Rivera allowed Miller to reach safely, putting runners at first and second. Midre Cummings ran for Miller, and Jay Bell tried to advance both runners with a bunt. Rivera made the play this time and retired Dellucci at third base.

Then, Tony Womack followed with a double to right field that scored Cummings and tied the game at 2-2. Bell advanced to third base on the hit, putting the winning run just 90 feet (27 meters) away from home plate.

Craig Counsell got hit by a pitch to load the bases and bring up Luis Gonzalez. The Yankees brought their infielders in to try to cut down the winning run on a grounder.

Gonzalez slapped a soft liner over Jeter's head at shortstop to drive in Bell with the winning run. The Arizona Diamondbacks were the world champions!

"It was like winning in the bottom of the ninth against God," Grace said in an article by Seth Livingstone for *USA Today*.

New York City Mayor Rudolph Giuliani, a die-hard Yankees fan, went to the Diamondbacks' locker room to offer his congratulations. "That was the greatest Game 7 ever," Giuliani said in an Associated Press article by Walker. "As a Yankees fan, I wish it turned out differently."

Johnson earned the victory, making him the first pitcher to win three times in a World Series since Mickey Lolich of the Detroit Tigers in 1968. "It seemed pretty surreal to me, watching this all develop," Johnson said after the game. "I just stood up on the top of the bench hoping we could get something strung together, and we did."

Johnson shared Most Valuable Player honors with Schilling. The duo combined to win four games and allowed just six earned runs in 38²/₃ innings while striking out 45 batters.

"We won it as a team. We beat the best closer in baseball and the best team in baseball," Schilling said in Livingstone's story. "I didn't say how we'd win it—just that we'd win it."

"Me and Curt fed off one another all year long," Johnson said. "And, you know, I think we made ourselves better."

For Johnson, it was the culmination of a lifelong dream. He piled up plenty of individual awards through his first 14 seasons in the major leagues. Finally, he was a champion and he would get to wear the championship ring for the rest of his life.

Better With Age

A sellout crowd of 47,025 was in attendance at Bank One Ballpark on April 1, 2002, to witness the unveiling of the Diamondbacks' World Series championship banner high above the swimming pool in right-center field.

Then, the fans were treated to another vintage performance by Randy Johnson.

In his first game in front of the home fans since he recorded the final four outs against the New York Yankees in Game 7 of the World Series five months earlier, the Big Unit was masterful once again.

Johnson tossed a six-hit shutout as the defending champions opened the season with a 2-0 victory over the San Diego Padres. Johnson struck out eight batters, walked only one, and improved his record to 5–0 in 10 opening-day starts.

"He's a freak of nature," Diamondback first baseman Mark Grace said in Bob Baum's article for The Associated Press. "It's a tribute to the shape he's in and the drive he has. He may be another Nolan Ryan and pitch until he's 45, because he's better now than he ever has been."

At 38 years old, Johnson proved right away that his fastball had not lost any velocity by consistently throwing in the 95- to 100-mile-per-hour range. His next-to-last pitch was clocked at 99 miles per hour (159 kilometers per hour) on the stadium radar gun, an amazing feat because pitchers usually tire at the end of games.

"If you can get stronger as the game progresses, a hitter doesn't really anticipate that," Johnson said in Baum's article. "He thinks that in the beginning or the middle of the game he's seen your best stuff."

Johnson was only getting started. The 2002 season turned out to be his best yet. He won a team-record and personal-best 24 games, lost only five, and had a 2.32 ERA while striking out 334 batters. Johnson led the league in wins, strikeouts, and ERA to earn his first career Triple Crown. He was just the second National League pitcher since 1973 to lead the league in all three categories, joining Dwight Gooden of the New York Mets who accomplished the feat in 1985.

Johnson was a unanimous choice for his fourth consecutive Cy Young Award, becoming the second pitcher ever and the first since Atlanta's Greg Maddux in 1995 to win four straight. He also became the first pitcher to have five straight seasons with 300 strikeouts. It was Johnson's sixth season altogether with more than 300 strikeouts, tying Nolan Ryan as the only two pitchers to have six in a career.

With the Diamondbacks fighting for first place in the final month of the season, Johnson took his performance to an incredible level. He was 5–0 with a 0.66 ERA in September, allowing just three earned runs in 41 innings pitched.

Jerry Colangelo, the managing general partner of the Arizona Diamondbacks, presented Randy Johnson with his third-straight Cy Young Award before the April 3, 2002, game against the San Diego Padres. In 2002, Johnson achieved his highest win total, 24, and earned another Cy Young Award.

Johnson's tremendous pitching helped the Diamondbacks win 98 games and edge the San Francisco Giants to capture the National League West championship.

But Arizona's hopes of repeating as world champions were dashed in the first round of the playoffs against the St. Louis Cardinals. Johnson could not maintain his late-season dominance in Game 1 against the Cardinals. He allowed six runs and 10 hits in six innings as St. Louis cruised to a 12-2 victory.

Curt Schilling pitched well for the Diamondbacks in Game 2, but the Cardinals won 2-1 and went on to complete a three-game sweep. It would be the last time Johnson pitched in the postseason with Arizona.

A DIFFICULT SEASON

The 2003 season was very frustrating for the Big Unit because of a right-knee injury that required surgery and twice landed him on the disabled list.

Johnson made only 18 starts and finished the season 6–8, just the third time he had a losing record. His ERA of 4.26 was the second-highest in his career.

Right from the start, Johnson did not seem like himself. He was 0–2 with an 8.31 ERA in his first three outings, before swelling in his knee forced him to go on the disabled list for the first time since 1996. Johnson returned to pitch against the New York Mets on April 27 in the second game of a doubleheader. He struck out 12 batters in six innings in a 7-3 victory but again was placed on the disabled list the next day.

On May 1, Johnson had arthroscopic surgery on his troublesome knee and missed 12 weeks of the season. During his rehabilitation period, Johnson refused to speak to reporters. He broke his silence after pitching against the San Diego Padres on July 20. Johnson gave up two runs—one earned—and six hits in six innings in a 3-2 loss.

"I was a little erratic, but for the most part I felt like I kept us in the ballgame," Johnson said in an article for The Associated Press by Bernie Wilson.

Few highlights filled the rest of the year for Johnson. He did achieve a first at the plate when he homered off Doug Davis of the Milwaukee Brewers on September 19. Nine days after turning 40, Johnson became the oldest player in major-league history to hit his first career home run.

After the 2003 season, the Diamondbacks traded Curt Schilling to the Boston Red Sox because the team needed to trim its payroll. The Diamondbacks were not going to have enough money to re-sign Schilling when he became a free agent at the end of the 2004 season. The deal broke up the Johnson-Schilling tandem, which had become one of the most feared duos in the league.

Without Schilling, the Diamondbacks relied heavily on Johnson in 2004. He rebounded nicely from his injury-shortened season and nearly won his sixth Cy Young Award. Johnson won 16 games but lost 14 mainly because the Diamondbacks' offense did not score a lot of runs when he pitched. Johnson finished with a 2.60 ERA. He led the majors in strikeouts for the ninth time with 290, finished second behind Houston's Roger Clemens in voting for the Cy Young Award, and was named to his tenth All-Star Game.

A SPECIAL GAME

His biggest accomplishment that season came on May 18, when he retired all 27 batters he faced in Arizona's 2-0 victory over the Atlanta Braves. In doing so, he became the oldest player—he was 40—in the history of the major leagues to pitch a perfect game.

"A game like this was pretty special," Johnson said in Paul Newberry's article for The Associated Press. "It doesn't come along very often."

Johnson could not resist poking fun at those who had said after the previous season that his best days were in the past. "Not bad for being 40 years old," he said.

☆ ☆ ☆ ☆ ☆ ☆

PERFECTION

From pitching a no-hitter to winning a World Series championship, Randy Johnson had nearly done it all in his brilliant career. On May 18, 2004, against the Atlanta Braves, Johnson accomplished the only feat he was missing: a perfect game.

The Big Unit retired all 27 batters he faced in Arizona's 2-0 victory over the Braves to record just the seventeenth perfect game in major-league history and the fifteenth since the modern era began in 1900.

At 40 years old, Johnson also became the oldest pitcher to throw a perfect game. Cy Young was 37 when he did it in 1904.

Johnson struck out 13 batters in a dominant performance. He only came close to walking one batter—Johnny Estrada in the second inning. With the count at 3–2, Estrada fouled off three straight pitches before he swung and missed.

The Braves hit several balls hard and had some close calls against Johnson. Atlanta's first hitter, Jesse Garcia, led off with a bunt toward first base and tried to reach with a headfirst slide, but Shea Hillenbrand made the tag. In the fifth inning, J. D. Drew hit a liner toward the right-field corner, but Danny Bautista made a basket catch.

With two outs in the sixth inning, Braves pitcher Mike Hampton hit a slow roller. Shortstop Alex Cintrón charged in and picked it up, and his throw to first base beat Hampton by a half-step. Johnson appreciated Cintrón's effort and gave him a pat with

Later that season, Johnson became the fourth pitcher to record 4,000 strikeouts in his career when he fanned San Diego's Jeff Cirillo in the eighth inning of a game on June 29.

★ ☆ ☆ ☆ ☆ ☆

his glove as he ran off the field. The crowd of 23,381 fans at Turner Field stopped cheering for the Braves and started rooting for Johnson by the end of the eighth inning.

Johnson retired Mark DeRosa on a grounder to second base for the first out in the ninth and struck out Nick Green looking for the second out. The next batter, Eddie Pérez, was no match for Johnson. Pérez struck out on a 98-mile-per-hour (158-kilometer-per-hour) fastball to end the game. Johnson pumped his fist and raised his glove in the air. Young catcher Robby Hammock greeted Johnson with a bear hug, and the rest of the team mobbed him while the Braves fans gave him a standing ovation and chanted, "Randy! Randy! Randy!"

It was the first perfect game in the majors since David Cone of the New York Yankees pitched one against Montreal on July 18, 1999. It also was the first no-hitter in the brief history of the Arizona Diamondbacks, who joined the league in 1998.

Johnson's only other no-hitter came for Seattle in 1990, giving him the longest span between a pair of no-hitters by a pitcher in baseball history. He became only the fifth pitcher to throw no-hitters in both the National and American Leagues, joining Young, Jim Bunning, Hideo Nomo, and Nolan Ryan. The most satisfying part for Johnson was proving that he still was a dominant pitcher after missing most of the 2003 season with a knee injury that required surgery.

A jubilant Randy Johnson celebrated with catcher Robby Hammock after completing a perfect game against the Atlanta Braves on May 18, 2004. At 40, Johnson was the oldest pitcher ever to throw a perfect game.

He passed Steve Carlton for third place on the all-time strikeout list and became first among left-handers by recording his 4,137th strikeout on September 15 against Colorado.

Despite Johnson's effort, the Diamondbacks had a terrible season. They went 51–111, recording the worst record in the National League since the Mets had the same mark in 1963.

Throughout the year, Johnson's name was mentioned in trade rumors. Arizona needed to rebuild its struggling team by adding prospects, so dealing Johnson was a logical way to get young players. Speculation that the Big Unit was heading to the New York Yankees began soon after the Red Sox acquired Schilling. The talk continued into spring training and persisted during the season until the trade deadline passed on July 31.

Johnson was in the first year of a two-year, $33 million contract extension he signed with Arizona, and his deal had a no-trade clause. If the Diamondbacks wanted to trade him, Johnson had the right to veto the move.

Yankees owner George Steinbrenner only added to the hype when he told a radio station in June how much he coveted Johnson. Steinbrenner told Sporting News Radio:

> God, who wouldn't love to have Randy Johnson? He's a dominator, and we'd love to have him. Anybody would love to have him, but I also know that [Diamondbacks managing general partner] Jerry Colangelo is not going to give him away. We'll have to see what happens as the deadline gets closer. We'll see. We will try and make a move somewhere along the line here. We are working on it feverishly. We are not going to mention any names, but we're looking. You can never have enough pitching.

The Yankees and the Diamondbacks could not agree on a trade during the season. Still, New York went to the playoffs.

The Yankees, though, not only failed to win the World Series that fall, they also became the first team in major-league history to lose a playoff series after winning the first three games.

Even worse, it was Schilling and the Red Sox who mounted the greatest comeback in baseball history, winning four straight games against the Yankees after losing the first three to capture the American League championship and advance to the World Series.

As the Red Sox went on to sweep St. Louis and celebrate their first championship in 86 years, the Yankees were devastated. If they had just found a way to get Johnson from the Diamondbacks, maybe they would have avoided an embarrassing collapse against their bitter rivals.

Steinbrenner and Yankees general manager Brian Cashman set their sights on making sure that Johnson would wear those famous blue pinstripes in 2005.

10

Big Unit in the Big Apple

With a history that includes some of the greatest players ever to appear in the major leagues and a long tradition of winning championships, the New York Yankees are commonly considered the most famous team in professional sports.

Babe Ruth, Lou Gehrig, Mickey Mantle, Joe DiMaggio, Roger Maris, Yogi Berra, Reggie Jackson, Derek Jeter, and Alex Rodriguez are just some of the players who have called Yankee Stadium home since the team began playing there in 1923.

For a long time, Yankees owner George Steinbrenner wanted to add Randy Johnson to that list of all-stars.

Soon after the Yankees lost to the rival Boston Red Sox in the 2004 American League Championship Series, acquiring

Johnson from the Arizona Diamondbacks became the top off-season priority for management.

Winning the Big Unit sweepstakes, though, would not be easy. The Diamondbacks wanted quality players in return, and Johnson still had to agree to waive his no-trade clause to accept a deal to New York.

After weeks of discussions between the two teams, The Associated Press reported on December 1, 2004, that the Yankees had ended trade talks because they felt that Arizona's asking price was too high.

AP baseball writer Ronald Blum wrote that New York proposed a deal that would send to the Diamondbacks right-hander Javier Vázquez, pitching prospect Brad Halsey, and a significant amount of money, believed to be $12 million to $13 million.

Blum, citing unidentified sources, reported that Arizona countered by asking the Yankees for Vázquez, Halsey, setup reliever Tom Gordon, and $18.5 million.

Two weeks later, the Yankees and Diamondbacks finally reached a tentative agreement that would send Johnson to New York. The Los Angeles Dodgers also were involved in the trade, which included several players being moved around. The Dodgers, though, withdrew from the proposed trade five days later, leaving Arizona and New York to try again to work out a deal with each other.

Finally, on December 30, the Yankees agreed to send the Diamondbacks Vázquez, Halsey, catcher Dioner Navarro, and $9 million for Johnson.

A week later, the Yankees reached a preliminary agreement with Johnson on a $32 million, two-year contract extension. Only one step remained to put the finishing touches on the drawn-out trade: The players involved had to pass their physicals.

This routine process turned a bit ugly for Johnson when he got into a confrontation on a Manhattan sidewalk with a television cameraman and a newspaper photographer on his way to the doctor's office for his physical on the morning of January 10, 2005.

It was Johnson's introduction to the intense media scrutiny in a major city like New York, and he handled it unprofessionally. Johnson apologized for his actions in a statement released later in the day, but he was off to a rocky start in the Big Apple.

The Yankees held a news conference the following day to officially introduce Johnson as the newest member of their team. Johnson opened the news conference by making a public apology.

The incident received tremendous attention in New York and across the country, earning Johnson criticism for his behavior. Soon, though, the focus shifted to Johnson's abilities on the mound and whether he had enough left in his arm to help the Yankees win another championship. Some in New York thought the 41-year-old Johnson was too far past his prime to make a difference. Others argued that he was the last piece the Yankees needed to regain their dominance.

IN THE ROTATION

Johnson joined a starting rotation that included Mike Mussina, Kevin Brown, Carl Pavano, and Jaret Wright. The formidable pitching staff helped make the Yankees the odds-on favorites to win it all heading into spring training.

Before he could be a true Yankee, Johnson had to look like one. That meant he had to conform with Steinbrenner's rules and trim his long hair and facial hair. Steinbrenner liked what he saw when he met Johnson for the first time after the trade.

Sitting at his locker in the clubhouse at the Yankees' practice facility in Tampa, Florida, Johnson was approached by Steinbrenner after a workout on February 18.

"Hi, big man," Steinbrenner said, according to an article by Blum for The Associated Press.

"How you doing, Mr. Steinbrenner?" Johnson responded.

"Glad you're here. Glad you're cleaned up, and glad you're here," Steinbrenner said.

☆ ☆ ☆ ☆ ☆

A BRONX WELCOME

The sellout crowd at Yankee Stadium started to cheer the minute Randy Johnson emerged from the dugout and walked out to the bullpen to start warming up, and they never stopped yelling for the Big Unit.

On a chilly Sunday night in the Bronx on April 3, 2005, Johnson made his much-anticipated debut with the New York Yankees. Fittingly, the Yankees were playing their biggest rival, the Boston Red Sox.

Only 5½ months earlier, the Red Sox had stunned the Yankees and the nation by coming back from a three-games-to-zero deficit in the American League Championship Series to win four straight games and advance to the World Series.

Johnson was New York's prized addition in the off-season, the pitcher who was expected to be the difference-maker for the Yankees in their quest to win a record twenty-seventh world championship.

In his first outing before the home fans, Johnson lived up to the high expectations. He pitched six innings, held the Red Sox to one run on five hits and struck out six batters. The Yankees won, 9-2.

"It was nice to kind of get a feeling of the way it's going to be here," Johnson said in an article by Mark Feinsand for MLB.com. "Obviously, I don't think tonight's going to be indicative of the way it's going to be every time I pitch, but I got it out of the way, playing Boston and my first start here at Yankee Stadium. It was a real nice effort by everybody."

Now that he had met the Boss's approval, Johnson had to make sure he impressed his new coaches and Manager Joe Torre. Certainly that would not be a problem for someone

☆ ☆ ☆ ☆ ☆

With 54,818 fans standing and screaming, Johnson blew a fastball by Johnny Damon on his first pitch. He retired the first three batters he faced, striking out Edgar Rentería and Manny Ramírez to end the inning.

"I had a lot of adrenaline in the first inning, and a lot of things really weren't working for me early in the game, other than my fastball," Johnson said in Feinsand's article. "I naturally want to establish that, but then as the game progressed, I was able to throw my breaking ball to my advantage."

Johnson got some help from his defense in the second inning after David Ortiz led off with a double. Kevin Millar followed with a drive to left field that appeared headed for the seats, but Hideki Matsui leaped at the wall and made the catch to prevent a two-run homer.

Jay Payton gave the Red Sox a 1-0 lead later in the inning with a run-scoring single, but Boston would not score again against Johnson. Meanwhile, the Yankees' offense got 10 hits and four runs in less than five innings against David Wells.

Working with a lead, Johnson did not let up. He struck out Ortiz in the fourth inning, fanned Damon in the fifth, and left two runners on to end the sixth. Johnson threw 95 pitches and exited with a 6-1 lead.

Yankee shortstop and captain Derek Jeter certainly was impressed. "You couldn't ask for a better performance from him," Jeter said in Feinsand's article. "He did exactly what we expected from him."

Ever competitive, Randy Johnson showed his reaction after retiring the side in the first inning of his first game as a New York Yankee. Johnson held the archrival Red Sox to one run in six innings, as New York went on to defeat Boston, 9-2, in its opener on April 3, 2005.

with such an impressive résumé, which included five Cy Young Awards, 10 trips to the All-Star Game, and a World Series co-MVP Award.

Later in the spring, Johnson was honored when Torre picked him to start the season opener against the Red Sox on April 3 at Yankee Stadium.

Fans cheered wildly when Johnson walked out to the bullpen to warm up for his Yankee debut on a chilly Sunday night in the Bronx. Johnson did not disappoint the sellout crowd, pitching six innings and allowing just one run and five hits. He also struck out six to help the Yankees beat the Red Sox, 9-2.

"I was pretty excited to go out there," Johnson said in an article by Blum for The Associated Press. "I guess I got a lot out of the way."

It was the first of 17 wins for Johnson in his first season with the Yankees. He lost only eight games and finished with a 3.79 ERA in 34 games. Johnson struggled with his mechanics throughout most of the season, but he regained his old form after discovering on video that he was rushing his delivery and dropping his arm. He went 6–0 with a 1.92 ERA in his final eight starts.

Johnson, however, could not help the Yankees win their twenty-seventh World Championship. The team with baseball's largest payroll, which exceeded $200 million, flopped again in the playoffs, losing to the Los Angeles Angels of Anaheim in the American League Division Series.

The series was tied at one game apiece when Johnson took the mound for Game 3 at Yankee Stadium. The Yankees brought Johnson to New York exactly for important games like this one.

Instead, he pitched poorly in his first playoff game in New York. Johnson lasted only three-plus innings against the Angels; he gave up nine hits and left with the Yankees trailing 5-0. New York rallied to take the lead, but eventually lost, 11-7.

Fans booed loudly when Johnson left the game, and the Big Unit said afterward that he did not blame them.

"If I would have paid for a ticket to watch me pitch today, I would have booed myself," Johnson said in an Associated Press article by Brian Mahoney.

He also gave the Angels credit. "They have a relentless team," Johnson said. "If you don't make your pitches, regardless of who you are, they're going to make you pay."

The Yankees won Game 4 to tie the series and force a decisive game back at Angel Stadium. Mussina got the start and allowed five runs in less than three innings before giving way to Johnson.

Pitching on just two days' rest, Johnson held the Angels scoreless for 4 1/3 innings. New York's hitters, however, could not overcome the early deficit, and the Angels eliminated the Yankees with a 5-3 victory.

Disappointed that the season ended prematurely, Johnson resolved to do his best to help the Yankees get back to the World Series in 2006.

ALL EYES ON RANDY

Johnson's private life was thrust into the spotlight during spring training when it became known that he had fathered a daughter during a relationship in his rookie season.

A report on the Web site *The Smoking Gun* in March said that Johnson was suing his former girlfriend Laurel Roszell for nearly $100,000 in payments made for day care for their daughter, Heather. In 1997, Johnson agreed to pay Laurel Roszell $5,000 a month in child support and $750 a month for day-care expenses. Johnson was suing to get back some of the day-care payments, saying that Heather, who was now 16, had not been in day care for at least five years.

"I do acknowledge that I have a daughter from a previous relationship, which ended years before my marriage," Johnson said in a statement. "I have fully financially supported her and have made every effort to protect her privacy." Johnson had met his daughter once, when she was still hospitalized after her birth, the Web site said.

Johnson did not let the news affect his performance. He was again chosen to start the Yankees' season opener, and he pitched well in a victory at Oakland on April 3.

Johnson, though, was clearly not the same dominant pitcher he had been during most of his career. The zip on his fastball was gone, and hitters had little trouble batting against him.

After losing to Boston on May 9, Johnson's record fell to 5–3 and his ERA was all the way up to 5.01.

"It looked like I didn't have a clue out there," Johnson said in an Associated Press article by Mike Fitzpatrick. "I'm throwing balls to the backstop and trying to overthrow, putting more pressure on myself. I can't remember the last time I pitched a good ball game."

The team was so concerned that it sent Johnson for an MRI exam on his left shoulder to make sure he was not hurt. Meanwhile, fans in New York were convinced that Johnson was nearing the end of his career.

The tests revealed nothing abnormal with Johnson's shoulder, so he remained in the starting rotation. Johnson continued to struggle, allowing more hits and runs than ever before. But a star-studded lineup gave Johnson plenty of offensive support, so he was able to win more games than he lost.

In mid-June, Johnson was suspended for five games by the commissioner's office for intentionally throwing at Eduardo Perez of the Cleveland Indians during a game in which Yankees catcher Jorge Posada was earlier hit by a pitch from Jason Johnson.

Randy Johnson appealed the suspension but dropped the appeal after his next start at Philadelphia. The Phillies won that game, but Johnson was encouraged after allowing three runs and five hits in seven innings. "I'm not as done as some people think I am," a confident Johnson told reporters.

The up-and-down season continued for Johnson, with his ERA stuck around 5.00 most of the year. New York's hitters,

☆ ☆ ☆ ☆ ☆ ☆
JOHNSON REACHES 4,500 STRIKEOUTS

Randy Johnson always put team goals ahead of personal accomplishments, so it was no surprise that he did not get too excited each time he set a record or reached another milestone.

On August 14, 2006, Johnson became the third pitcher in major-league history to reach 4,500 strikeouts. He was more pleased, though, that his pitching performance helped the New York Yankees beat the Los Angeles Angels of Anaheim, 7-2, that night to extend their lead in the American League East to two games over Boston.

"I've never allowed myself to get too caught up in the accomplishments. Maybe I will when I'm done," Johnson said in an article by Mike Fitzpatrick for The Associated Press.

Johnson pitched seven innings against the Angels. He allowed two runs and eight hits and fanned five. The Big Unit struck out Tim Salmon in the fourth inning for No. 4,500. Only Hall of Famer Nolan Ryan (5,714) and Roger Clemens (who had 4,604 strikeouts at the end of the 2006 season) are ahead of Johnson on the all-time strikeout list.

"Randy is a dominant pitcher," Yankees manager Joe Torre said in Ryan Mink's article for MLB.com. "He has been a dominant pitcher for a long, long, long time. Not too many guys of his age—Nolan Ryan did it—dominate the game into their 40s. And Roger (Clemens), of course, is doing it."

After Johnson struck out Salmon, the crowd at Yankee Stadium chanted, "Randy! Randy!" Catcher Jorge Posada tossed

though, continually bailed him out by scoring a lot of runs when he pitched.

Johnson achieved another milestone on August 14, when he became the third pitcher in major-league history to reach

☆ ☆ ☆ ☆ ☆ ☆

the ball into the dugout to be kept as a souvenir and came out from behind the plate to stop the game momentarily.

According to Mink, Posada said: "I went out there and said, 'Congratulations, you've done a hell of a job. You deserve it. You deserve this ovation. Enjoy it.'"

Johnson retired the next batter to finish the inning and waved to his family behind home plate as he walked off the field.

In Mink's article, Johnson said: "I could not strike out anybody for the rest of my career, and I'd be content. Winning ball games is really how you measure a pitcher, not by strikeouts. Today's game was a by-product of what I've done over the majority of my career, and that was started in Seattle and really ended in Arizona."

In his previous outing, Johnson was nine outs away from his third career no-hitter before Tadahito Iguchi of the Chicago White Sox lined a single to left field to lead off the seventh inning.

On June 29, 2004, Johnson, pitching for Arizona, struck out San Diego's Jeff Cirillo for No. 4,000. The Padres won the game, 3-2.

On the day he celebrated his thirty-seventh birthday, Johnson fanned Florida's Mike Lowell on September 10, 2000, to join Hall of Fame pitcher Steve Carlton as the only left-handers to have 3,000 career strikeouts. In that game, Johnson also reached 300 strikeouts for the season, tying him with Ryan for accomplishing the feat three consecutive years.

Johnson broke that mark by getting 300 strikeouts in 2001 and 2002 to make it five straight years.

The scoreboard at Yankee Stadium flashes Randy Johnson's latest accomplishment—his 4,500th strikeout. The milestone came against Tim Salmon of the Angels on August 14, 2006. Heading into the 2007 season, Johnson was third on the all-time career strikeout list, behind Nolan Ryan and Roger Clemens.

4,500 strikeouts. He fanned Tim Salmon of the Angels in the fourth inning of that game to reach the mark.

"It means I've been around a long time and I've struck out a lot of batters," Johnson said in an Associated Press article by Fitzpatrick. "That's probably why my arm's pretty tired."

Johnson had a string of three straight solid outings late in the year, but he ended the regular season with a loss against the Tampa Bay Devil Rays. His season record was 17–11 with a 5.00 ERA.

The Yankees clinched their ninth-straight American League East title on September 20, so Johnson had another chance to pitch in the playoffs and try to help his team win the World Series.

THE POSTSEASON

Hardly anyone gave the Detroit Tigers a chance to beat the mighty Yankees in the first round of the playoffs. After all, the Tigers were just three years removed from a terrible season in which they lost 119 games. And these were the Yankees, with their $200 million-plus payroll and a lineup filled with star players from top to bottom.

It appeared New York would have an easy time with the Tigers after an 8-4 victory at Yankee Stadium in Game 1 of the best-of-five series. But upstart Detroit rallied to win the next one, 4-3, and set up a pivotal Game 3 back at home.

Once again, Johnson would be called upon to pitch a crucial playoff game for the Yankees. He was ineffective in his Game 3 start against the Angels a year earlier in a series that New York lost in five games. The Big Unit and the Yankees desperately needed a solid performance against a young team that was playing with a lot of excitement and emotion in the first playoff game in Detroit since 1987.

On the day of the game, a *New York Post* headline above a story written by columnist Joel Sherman read: "Yet another chance for Johnson to earn his stripes." Sherman began his story:

> We know now that Randy Johnson is never going to be the pitcher the Yankees thought they were obtaining, an April-through-October dominator. That is fine now. They don't need that today. All they need is for him to be better than Kenny Rogers. A lot better. The Yankees are now in the same precarious spot as last year, tied at a game apiece in the Division Series and—on paper anyway—having a huge Game 3 starting pitching edge. But in Game 3 last year, the

Angels' Paul Byrd pitched poorly, yet Johnson was even worse. The Yankees lost, when victory very likely would have meant advancement rather than the first-round ouster they suffered.

The pressure certainly was on Johnson to pitch well. He had not lived up to expectations in his other playoff outing with the Yankees and now he had a chance to redeem himself. But Johnson was not completely healthy going into the play-offs. He almost did not get an opportunity to pitch after he was diagnosed with a herniated disc in his back late in the regular season. Johnson decided to get an epidural shot to ease the pain and continue pitching.

It proved to be a bad idea. Johnson struggled against the Tigers on a 50°F (10°C) night. He gave up three runs in the second inning as the Yankees fell behind 3-0. Meanwhile, the 41-year-old Rogers pitched brilliantly for Detroit. Johnson gave up two more runs in the sixth inning and left the game trailing 5-0. Rogers did not allow a run, shutting down the dangerous Yankee hitters to give the Tigers a two-games-to-one series lead and put the Yankees on the brink of elimination.

For the second straight year, Johnson failed to deliver in his most important start. A day later, the Tigers beat the Yankees to complete a shocking upset.

Fans in New York certainly expected more from Johnson and the Yankees, especially against the Tigers. Steinbrenner was angry that his team fell short again, calling the result "absolutely not acceptable" and "a sad failure."

Making matters worse for Johnson, he learned a short time later that he would need surgery to repair the herniated disc in his back. Johnson had the same operation in 1996, but he was 10 years younger then. He made a complete recovery and pitched successfully. Now he had to do it all over again.

BACK TO THE DESERT

When Johnson pulled off his pinstriped uniform after the Yankees lost to the Tigers, he could not have known that he would not be putting it back on again in a few months.

Instead, Johnson's next jersey would be a very familiar one. In early January 2007, the Yankees and the Diamondbacks agreed to a trade that sent the Big Unit back to Arizona. Johnson would no longer have to deal with the intense media scrutiny in the Big Apple and the pressure of playing for the Yankees. Rather, he could close out his long, distinguished career in the desert wearing the new red-trimmed uniform of the Diamondbacks.

Even though Johnson was coming off back surgery and had not been the dominant pitcher he used to be, the Diamondbacks gave the 43-year-old a two-year contract worth $26 million. Arizona also traded right-handed reliever Luis Vizcaíno and three minor leaguers to the Yankees: right-handers Ross Ohlendorf and Steven Jackson and shortstop Alberto Gonzalez.

"A lot of people say my career is over," Johnson said at the news conference reintroducing him in Arizona. "I had a 5.00 ERA. Well, I was out there pitching with a bad back for most of the year.

"Ten years ago, I had back surgery, and they thought my career was over then. When I walk around with a chip on my shoulder, it's because it's been an uphill battle. I've always had to prove my worth, I guess you would say, much like now."

Johnson had surgery on his back in October, passed his physical when he was traded, and started to play catch and to throw off a mound before spring training began in February.

He smiled quite a bit while talking to reporters and seemed relieved that his days with the Yankees were over. Johnson insisted, however, that he had no regrets about going to New York. "The run that I had, as short-lived as it was, as well-documented as it was in New York, I wouldn't change a thing,"

Randy Johnson stretched his back during a spring-training game on March 29, 2007, between the Arizona Diamondbacks and the San Diego Padres. After the 2006 season, Johnson was traded to the Diamondbacks, and he had surgery on a herniated disc in his back.

Johnson said. "I think those are life experiences that make a man. I made some mistakes there; I fessed up to the mistakes that I made. On the field, I gave everything I had."

During his two seasons with the Yankees, Johnson won 34 games but none in the postseason. Johnson never came close to becoming a fan favorite like Derek Jeter and others in New York, but he said he "never got the feeling" that the Yankee fans wanted him gone.

"As a consumer myself, when I buy a steak or go to the movies, if it's not a good steak I send it back and if it's not a good movie I usually leave," Johnson said. "If I didn't pitch well there, they'd boo me. I've been booed here in a Diamondback uniform. It's completely understandable. That didn't bother me."

Johnson enjoyed his greatest success in Arizona, where he went 103–49 in six seasons and won four National League Cy Young Awards. He entered the 2007 season needing 20 victories to join the elite 300-win club.

Unlike the Yankees, the Diamondbacks are a younger team with less expectations. Johnson might be a better fit in Arizona's youth movement than with the star-laden Yankees.

"I'm excited about being back here to finish my career, absolutely," Johnson said. "Seems like youth has been a big thing here. Well, maybe this will be a fountain of youth coming back here and playing with a lot of young players."

STATISTICS

RANDY JOHNSON
Primary position: Pitcher

Full name: Randall David Johnson
Born: September 10, 1963, Walnut Creek,
California • Height: 6'10" • Weight: 225 lbs.
Teams: Montreal Expos (1988–1989);
Seattle Mariners (1989–1998); Houston
Astros (1998); Arizona Diamondbacks
(1999–2004); New York Yankees (2005–
2006); Arizona Diamondbacks (2007–)

★ ★ ★ ★ ★ ☆

YEAR	TEAM	G	W-L	ERA	SO	BB
1988	MON	4	3–0	2.42	25	7
1989	MON/SEA	29	7–13	4.82	130	96
1990	SEA	33	14–11	3.65	194	120
1991	SEA	33	13–10	3.98	228	152
1992	SEA	31	12–14	3.77	241	144
1993	SEA	35	19–8	3.24	308	99
1994	SEA	23	13–6	3.19	204	72
1995	SEA	30	18–2	2.48	294	65
1996	SEA	14	5–0	3.67	85	25
1997	SEA	30	20–4	2.28	291	77
1998	SEA/HOU	34	19–11	3.28	329	86
1999	ARI	35	17–9	2.48	364	70
2000	ARI	35	19–7	2.64	347	76
2001	ARI	35	21–6	2.49	372	71

Key: MON = Montreal Expos; SEA = Seattle Mariners; HOU = Houston Astros; ARI =
Arizona Diamondbacks; NYY = New York Yankees; G = Games; W–L = Wins-Losses;
ERA = Earned-run average; SO = Strikeouts; BB = Bases on balls

★ ★ ★ ★ ★

YEAR	TEAM	G	W-L	ERA	SO	BB
2002	ARI	35	24–5	2.32	334	71
2003	ARI	18	6–8	4.26	125	27
2004	ARI	35	16–14	2.60	290	44
2005	NYY	34	17–8	3.79	211	47
2006	NYY	33	17–11	5.00	172	60
TOTALS		556	280–147	3.22	4,544	1,409

Key: MON = Montreal Expos; SEA = Seattle Mariners; HOU = Houston Astros; ARI = Arizona Diamondbacks; NYY = New York Yankees; G = Games; W-L = Wins-Losses; ERA = Earned-run average; SO = Strikeouts; BB = Bases on balls

CHRONOLOGY

1963   September 10   Is born Randall David Johnson in Walnut Creek, California.

1978–1982   Attends Livermore High School in California, where he stars in baseball.

1982   Throws a perfect game in his last high school start.

Drafted in the third round by the Atlanta Braves but decides to go to college instead.

1982–1985   Plays baseball and basketball for the University of Southern California, attending college on an athletic scholarship.

1985   Drafted by the Montreal Expos in the second round.

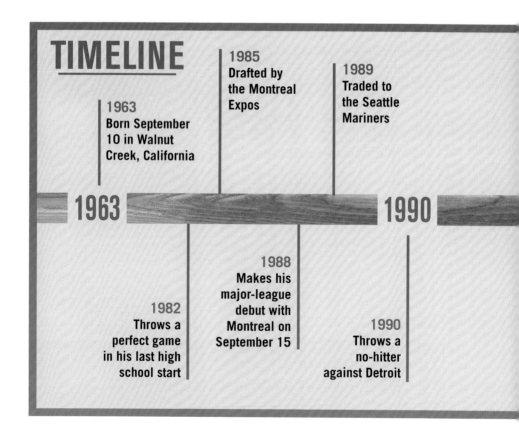

TIMELINE

1963 Born September 10 in Walnut Creek, California

1985 Drafted by the Montreal Expos

1989 Traded to the Seattle Mariners

1963

1990

1982 Throws a perfect game in his last high school start

1988 Makes his major-league debut with Montreal on September 15

1990 Throws a no-hitter against Detroit

1985–1988   Plays for three years in the minor leagues.

1988   **September 15** Makes his major-league debut with Montreal and earns his first major-league win.

1989   **May 25** Traded to the Seattle Mariners; wins first game for the Mariners against the Yankees on May 30.

September 4 Daughter Heather Roszell is born.

1990   **June 2** Throws a no-hitter against Detroit.

Makes his first All-Star team.

His photography is featured in Art Expo '90 in Los Angeles.

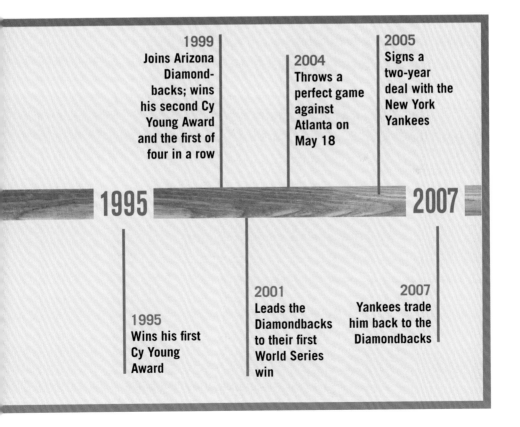

1999
Joins Arizona Diamond-backs; wins his second Cy Young Award and the first of four in a row

2004
Throws a perfect game against Atlanta on May 18

2005
Signs a two-year deal with the New York Yankees

1995

2007

1995
Wins his first Cy Young Award

2001
Leads the Diamondbacks to their first World Series win

2007
Yankees trade him back to the Diamondbacks

1992   Becomes the third Mariners pitcher to win the American League strikeout crown.

1993   Becomes a born-again Christian after the death of his father on Christmas Day the year before.

Marries wife Lisa.

Leads American League again in strikeouts.

1994   December 28 Daughter Samantha is born.

1995   Helps Seattle reach the playoffs; Mariners defeat the Yankees in the first round but lose to the Cleveland Indians in the American League Championship Series.

Wins his first Cy Young Award.

1996   April 5 Son Tanner is born.

Misses most of the season with a back injury.

1997   Sets a Seattle franchise record with 20 wins.

1998   April 23 Daughter Willow is born.

July 31 Traded to the Houston Astros and helps the Astros reach the playoffs.

1999   Plays his first season with Arizona after signing a four-year, $52.4 million contract.

Wins his second Cy Young Award and the first of four in a row.

December 4 Daughter Alexandria is born.

Receives the Bronze Sierra for his charity work to help combat cystic fibrosis.

2000   Wins the Cy Young Award.

2001   March 24 Kills a dove with a wild pitch in a freak accident that makes headlines.

May 8 Strikes out 20 batters in nine innings of an 11-inning game against the Cincinnati Reds.

Wins the Cy Young Award and leads the Diamondbacks to their first World Series win; is named the World Series Co-Most Valuable Player along with teammate Curt Schilling.

Named 2001 *Sports Illustrated* Co-Sportsman of the Year (shared with Schilling).

2002　Wins the Cy Young Award and leads the league in wins, ERA, and strikeouts (known as the "Triple Crown").

2003　Undergoes knee surgery.

2004　**May 18**　Throws a perfect game against Atlanta.

　　　June 29　Strikes out Jeff Cirillo of the San Diego Padres to become only the fourth pitcher to throw 4,000 strikeouts in a career.

2005　**January 11**　Signs a two-year, $32 million deal with the New York Yankees.

　　　Wins 17 games in his first season with the Yankees.

2006　**August 14**　Strikes out Tim Salmon of the Los Angeles Angels of Anaheim to record his 4,500th strikeout.

2007　**January 8**　Traded by the New York Yankees back to the Arizona Diamondbacks.

GLOSSARY

base on balls   When a batter takes four pitches out of the strike zone, the batter receives a base on balls, also called a walk, and is awarded first base.

basket catch   A catch of a fly ball to the outfield with an open glove near the belt level. It was Willie Mays's signature catch.

bullpen   The area where pitchers and catchers warm up. The bullpen is usually behind the outfield fences or off to the side along the left- or right-field line.

bunt   A ball not fully hit, with the batter either intending to get to first base before the infielder can field the ball or allowing an existing base runner to advance a base.

changeup   A pitch meant to look like a fastball but with less velocity.

closer   A relief pitcher who is consistently used to "close," or finish the game by getting the final outs.

complete game   A statistic credited to a pitcher who starts and finishes a game; the game may be shorter than nine innings if it is ruled a regulation game.

curveball   A pitch that curves on its way to the plate, thanks to the spin a pitcher places on the ball when throwing. Also known as a "breaking ball."

disabled list   Teams may remove injured players from their rosters by placing them temporarily on "the disabled list." Another player can then be called up as a replacement.

doubleheader   Two baseball games played by the same teams on the same day.

double play   A play by the defense during which two offensive players are put out in a continuous action. A typical combination is a ground ball to the shortstop, who throws to second base to get one runner out. The second baseman then throws to the first baseman to get the batter out.

dugout   The area where the players and managers not on the field can wait and watch. It usually has a bench with a roof, and in the major leagues includes a bat rack, glove and towel holders, a water cooler, a telephone to the bullpen, and more.

earned run   A run charged to a pitcher because a base runner who scores reached base on a hit or a walk allowed by the pitcher. The run must be scored without errors by defensive players.

earned-run average (ERA)   The number of earned runs that a pitcher allows every nine innings. It is computed by multiplying the total number of earned runs by nine and dividing by the number of innings pitched.

error   When a defensive player makes a mistake resulting in a runner reaching base, or advancing a base, an error is designated by the game's scorer.

farm team   A team that provides training and experience for young players, with the expectation that successful players will move to the major leagues.

fielder's choice   The fielder, upon fielding a batted ball, chooses to try to put out a base runner, allowing the batter to advance to first base. Despite reaching first safely, the batter is not credited with a hit and is charged with an at-bat.

free agent   A professional athlete who is free to negotiate a contract with any team.

grounder   A batted ball that hits the ground one or more times before reaching an infielder or leaving the infield.

loss   A loss is charged to the pitcher for the losing team who allows the run that gives the opposing team a lead they do not relinquish. The loss goes to the pitcher who

allowed the run-scoring player to reach base. A pitcher
need only face one batter to be charged with a loss.

no-hitter   A game in which one team does not get any hits;
a rare feat for a pitcher.

perfect game   A special no-hitter in which each batter is
retired consecutively, allowing no base runners through
walks, errors, or any other means.

quality start   A statistic credited to a starting pitcher who
allows three runs or less and pitches six innings or more.

relief pitcher   A pitcher brought in to substitute for (or
"relieve") another pitcher.

save   A statistic credited to a pitcher who comes into the
game with his team leading and completes the game without giving up the lead. The pitcher must be the last pitcher
in the game and must fulfill at least one of the following
conditions: He comes into the game with a lead of no more
than three runs and pitches at least one full inning; he
comes into the game with the potential tying or winning
run on base, at bat, or on deck; he pitches effectively for at
least three innings after entering the game.

setup reliever   A relief pitcher who is consistently used
before the closer.

shutout   A statistic credited to a pitcher who starts and finishes a game in which the opponents do not score a run.

strikeout   The retiring of a batter on three strikes.

wild pitch   A pitched ball that gets past a catcher and allows
runners to advance and that, in the opinion of the official
scorer, cannot be caught by the catcher.

win   A win is generally credited to the pitcher on the winning team who was in the game when his team last took
the lead. A starting pitcher must pitch at least five complete
innings to earn a win.

BIBLIOGRAPHY

The Associated Press. "Randy Johnson Kills Dove With Pitch," March 25, 2001.

The Associated Press. "Randy Johnson Had Pretty Much Done It All: Cy Young Awards, a No-Hitter, Strikeout Records, a World Series Championship," May 19, 2004.

The Associated Press. "Hey, Randy, Welcome to New York!" January 11, 2005.

Baum, Bob. "Diamondbacks 2, Padres 0." The Associated Press Archives, July 20, 2002.

———. "Diamondbacks Make Johnson Baseball's Highest-Paid Pitcher." The Associated Press Archives, November 30, 1998.

———. "Diamondbacks 2, Braves 0." The Associated Press Archives, May 18, 2004.

Blum, Ronald. "NewsBreak: Yankees Tell Diamondbacks They're Out of Johnson Trade Talks." The Associated Press Archives, January 11, 2004.

———. "Unit Meets Boss, Probably Will Start Opener Against Red Sox." The Associated Press Archives, February 16, 2005.

———. "Johnson Signs With Diamondbacks, Belle With Orioles." The Associated Press Archives, November 30, 1998.

———. "Schilling and Johnson Co-MVPs." The Associated Press Archives, November 4, 2001.

Borden, Sam. "Long Day for a Tall Yankee." *New York Daily News*, January 11, 2005.

Brookover, Bob. "Johnson Takes Game to Another Level." ESPN.com, May 15, 2000. Available online at *http://espn. starwave.com/mlb/s/2000/0510/525218.html*.

Campbell, Murray. "Johnson Kills Dove." *Globe and Mail* (Toronto), March 25, 2001.

Cour, Jim. "Johnson Gets an L to Go With His Ks." The Associated Press Archives, June 24, 1997.

———. "Tigers-Mariners." The Associated Press Archives, June 2, 1990.

Christopher, Matt. *On the Mound with Randy Johnson.* New York: Little, Brown & Company, 1998.

Feinsand, Mark. "Yanks Open Season With Win Over Sox." MLB.com. April 4, 2005. Available online at *http://www.mlb.com/content/printer_friendly/nyy/y2005/m04/d03/c998732.jsp.*

Fitzpatrick, Mike. "At Yankees News Conference, Johnson Apologizes for Run-In." The Associated Press Archives, February 18, 2005.

———. "Yankees 7, Angels 2." The Associated Press Archives, August 14, 2006.

———. *New York Daily News.* Available online at *http://www.nydailynews.com/front/story/270115p-231266c.html#q1.*

"Kruk Faces Johnson, All-Star Game." Video Replay. Available online at *http://mlb.mlb.com/NASApp/mlb/mlb/history/mlb_asgrecaps_story_headline.jsp?story_page=recap_1993.*

Livingstone, Seth. "World Series Good for Baseball and America." *USA Today Baseball Weekly,* November 5, 2001.

Lozano, Emmanuel. "Arizona First-Base Coach Eddie Rodriguez and Luis Gonzalez Celebrate the Hit That Finally Unseated the Yankees." *Arizona Republic,* November 5, 2001.

Mahoney, Brian. "Johnson Flops in Postseason Debut for Yankees." The Associated Press Archives, October 8, 2005.

Mink, Ryan. "Johnson Earns 4,500th Career Strikeout." MLB.com, August 14, 2006. Available online at *http://mlb.mlb.com/news/article.jsp?ymd=20060814&content_id=1610343&vkey=news_nyy&fext=.jsp&c_id=nyy.*

Newberry, Paul. "Diamondbacks 2, Braves 0." The Associated Press Archives, May 18, 2004.

"Randy Johnson." JockBio.com. Available online at *http://www.jockbio.com/Bios/RJohnson/RJohnson_bio.html.*

Reisner, Mel. "Diamondbacks 4, Reds 3, 11 innings." The Associated Press Archives, May 8, 2001.

Stone, Larry. *Randy Johnson: Arizona Heat!* Champaign, Ill.: Sports Publishing, Inc. 1999.

Walker, Ben. "Diamondbacks 15, Yankees 2." The Associated Press Archives, November 3, 2001.

———. "Diamondbacks 4, Yankees 0." The Associated Press Archives, October 28, 2001.

FURTHER READING

Bonner, Mike. *Randy Johnson: Baseball Legends.* Philadelphia, Pa.: Chelsea House Publishers, 1999.

Johnson, Randy, and Jim Rosenthal. *Randy Johnson's Power Pitching: The Big Unit's Secrets to Domination, Intimidation, and Winning.* New York: Three Rivers Press, 2003.

Stewart, Mark. *Randy Johnson: The Big Unit.* New York: Children's Press, 1998.

WEB SITES

Baseball Almanac

http://www.baseball-almanac.com

Baseball Reference

http://www.baseball-reference.com

Major League Baseball: The Official Site

http://mlb.mlb.com/index.jsp

The Official Site of the Arizona Diamondbacks

http://arizona.diamondbacks.mlb.com/index.jsp?c_id=ari

Randy Johnson's Official Web site

http://www.randy-johnson.com

PICTURE CREDITS

INDEX

ABOUT THE AUTHORS

SUSAN MUADDI DARRAJ is associate professor of English at Harford Community College in Bel Air, Maryland. She is the author of *The Inheritance of Exile*, published by University of Notre Dame Press.

ROB MAADDI is the Philadelphia sports editor/sports writer for The Associated Press. He is also host of *The Rob Maaddi Show* on ESPN Radio 920-AM in Philadelphia.